TELECOMPETITION

TELECOMPETITION

THE FREE MARKET ROAD TO THE INFORMATION HIGHWAY

LAWRENCE GASMAN

CATO INSTITUTE
Washington D.C.

Library of Congress Cataloging-in-Publication Data

Gasman, Lawrence.
    Telecompetition : the free market road to the information highway
Lawrence Gasman.
        p.   cm.
    Includes bibliographical references and index.
    ISBN 1-882577-08-6 — ISBN 1-882577-09-4 (pbk.)
    1. Telecommunication—United States—Deregulation.
2. Telecommunication policy—United States.   3. Competition—
United States.   I. Title
HE7781.G37 1994
388'.068—dc20   93-48497
                                                                  CIP

Cover Design by Colin Moore.

Printed in the United States of America.

CATO INSTITUTE
1000 Massachusetts Ave., N.W.
Washington, D.C. 20001

Contents

Preface

For the past decade I have been assessing the business opportunities that flow from new technologies, particularly new communications technologies. My academic background provided me with the intellectual tools of a business analyst, but my knowledge of the telecommunications industry in the United States is largely self-taught. As that self-education process proceeded, I frequently found myself asking whether what I had just read or heard about communications policy was "for real." Many of the laws and regulations governing telecommunications seemed baroque beyond all understanding; some seemed to fly in the face of everything I knew about economics.

I have come to understand that telecommunications policy in the United States really is as bad as it seems, and as the impact of profound technological change has been felt throughout the industry, the policy environment has become even more chaotic. At best, telecommunications policy is built on antiquated doctrines; at worst it is driven by whatever special communications interest happens to have the most political influence at a given time. Such an approach is neither a very intelligent way of making policy nor an effective means of serving the public interest.

This book represents the results of my deliberations on the goals and future of telecommunications policy. My basic conclusion is that traditional government policies covering electronic communications in the United States have been based on several key assumptions that no longer apply in what is coming to be known as the Information Age. Once those assumptions are abandoned, little if any justification remains for government intervention in the market for electronic communications services and products. Indeed, continued government interference in electronic communications markets can only exacerbate existing distortions and erode both economic and political liberties.

Given the immense complexity that generally marks any detailed discussion of electronic communications, my rather straightforward conclusions may appear simplistic. In my view, however, much of the apparent complexity associated with telecommunications debates is not intrinsic. That is, the complexity is not a function of the technology or of the marketplace, but is rather a consequence of regulation.

It is true, of course, that rapidly changing telecommunications technology is driving dramatic social change. Much of the economic restructuring now taking place is a result of the need to transform our present industrial society into an information-based postindustrial society in which communications will play an expanding role. But existing laws and regulations are making that process more complicated than it has to be. Regulators and lawmakers are notoriously sluggish beasts, and suggestions that they can keep pace with the current rate of change are simply not to be taken seriously. Although the laws and regulations governing electronic communications generally began simply enough, they have metastasized into a body of doctrine that can be manipulated by vested interests. Further, the costs imposed on consumers frequently far outweigh any benefits the original regulations might have provided. That in itself is an argument for radical deregulation.

In this book, I attempt to show that the information technology revolution calls for an equally revolutionary political and regulatory response. I begin with a sketch of the key developments in information technology. Chapter 2 highlights the clash that has developed between the philosophical underpinnings of U.S. telecommunications policy and the patterns of technological change in electronic communications. In particular, as the technologies of broadcasting, telephone communications, and publishing have converged, many of the fundamental distinctions inherent in almost all thinking about telecommunications policy have begun to evaporate.

My argument is not in itself particularly novel. Indeed students of telecommunications policy will immediately recognize the influence of the late Ithiel de Sola Pool.[1] The usual response to technological convergence from both federal and state policymakers is, however, a call for new legislation that will somehow preserve old

[1] De Sola Pool's work in this area is most widely accessible in Ithiel de Sola Pool, *Technologies of Freedom* (Cambridge, Mass.: Harvard University Press, 1983).

policy objectives. From the perspective of consumers of telecommunications services, such efforts are a total waste of time. Chapter 3 argues that well-meaning efforts by legislators and regulators to protect consumers from supposedly wicked acts by monopolists tend instead to preserve monopolies. By preventing the appearance of new services that might benefit business and residential customers, regulatory protection ends up protecting communications companies rather than end users. In fact, the whole notion of a communications monopoly is popularly misconceived, as chapter 3 explains.

Chapter 4 discusses another misconception—the idea that the radio spectrum is a scarce resource that needs to be allocated by a government agency. Attempts to continue down this road in the face of new technology will serve again only to preserve vested interests and slow the pace of useful service development.

Chapter 5 examines the consequences of an expanded role of the government in the development of a national communications infrastructure. Government decisionmakers simply do not possess enough commercial or technological knowledge to make useful decisions. This seems quite obvious to me, but "investments" in the communications infrastructure are one of the hottest topics being discussed by lawmakers on Capitol Hill and by bureaucrats at both the Federal Communications Commission and the Department of Commerce.

I turn finally to policy recommendations. In chapters 6 and 7, I essentially urge the government to do as little as possible. These final two chapters define what I think that "little" should be in both domestic and international communications policy, and I describe how the federal government might go about doing it.

Because this book is primarily a complaint about the continued overregulation of U.S. electronic communications, it is perhaps only fair to acknowledge how far we have come down the deregulatory road. Peter Huber has pointed out that the FCC's 1968 "Carterfone" decision was at the time considered a "regulatory frolic, going nowhere fast."[2] Yet Carterfone is now viewed as a key decision in the history of telephone company deregulation, leading to the

[2]Peter Huber, "The New Competitive Environment," *Society* 26 (July/August 1989): 27.

freedom, now taken for granted, to buy telephone equipment from anyone we choose. In the same article, Huber also observed, "In 1978, a great many people were certain that the whole idea of long-distance competition was another piece of regulatory insanity."[3] Long-distance competition not only exists, of course, but deregulation in that area has greatly benefited both business and residential consumers.[4]

The belief that telecommunications deregulation was supported only by a fringe group of Hayek and Mises disciples may have contributed in a minor way to AT&T's stubborn defense of the status quo. The memoirs of the Bell executives who bitterly fought increased market discipline and divestiture are the stories of men who apparently genuinely believed they were heroes, fighting the good fight to preserve the so-called national treasure that was the Bell system from the evils of laissez faire.[5]

Although Ma Bell did some distinctly unmotherly things during her campaign to preserve her far-flung monopolies, the fight for telephone deregulation has still been less emotive than the deregulatory fight in the broadcasting industry.[6] Consider comments about Mark Fowler, who as chairman of the FCC during the Reagan administration was an ardent supporter of broadcasting deregulation. Brownstein and Easton, in a book emanating from the Ralph Nader organization, quoted "a prominent D.C. communications attorney" as saying of Fowler, "His views are absolutely wild, way out."[7] The authors went on to cite Les Brown, editor of *Channels* magazine and former television reporter for the *New York Times*, who remarked, "I fear Mark Fowler because he doesn't know what he is talking about and is eager to turn his words into action."[8]

---

[3]Ibid.

[4]Such comments are very comforting to those of us who believe—unlike the mainstream—that communications deregulation still has a long way to go.

[5]See, for example, W. Brooke Tunstall, *Disconnecting Parties* (New York: McGraw-Hill, 1985) or Alvin von Auw, *Heritage and Destiny* (New York: Praeger, 1983).

[6]That may be in part because broadcasting policy debates almost always become entangled with First Amendment issues.

[7]Ronald Brownstein and Nina Easton, *Reagan's Ruling Class* (New York: Pantheon, 1982), p. 693.

[8]Ibid.

Despite the success of deregulatory efforts, such attitudes are not necessarily a thing of the past. I attended a meeting at which Alfred Sikes, the chairman of the FCC under President Bush, defended the need for deregulation but then reasserted the supposed right of the FCC to control broadcasting content with regard to material that is thought to be pornographic. In my own work, I find myself bombarded with self-serving material from communications companies asserting that "free" communications markets require government restraints on their competitors. Not only are legislators and regulators in Washington apparently convinced by such arguments, but they are also impressed by the industrial-policy myth that calls for government subsidies of high-definition television, information superhighways, and other communications technologies.

Over the four years that I have worked on this book, there has been a significant slowing of the general pace of communications deregulation. The decision to allow the Bell companies to enter the information services business is a significant victory, but even that move is being challenged by some lawmakers. Meanwhile, legislation that would reregulate the cable television industry has been passed. Such developments indicate a need to defend the doctrine that free markets in electronic communications goods and services ultimately benefit everyone, and that "hands-off" may be the best telecommunications policy of all.

In all fairness, many of the people who have made this book possible, especially my clients and colleagues in the telecommunications industry, may not share my views. Despite differences in our views, however, I would like to offer a collective thanks to everyone who has helped me in this project—both knowingly and unwittingly—by helping me understand how the telecommunications world works. I especially want to thank David Boaz and Catherine England at the Cato Institute for providing me with the opportunity to write this book. Catherine in particular deserves special mention for being unbelievably patient with me and with a project that was supposed to take months, not years.

Finally, while on the topic of patience, my deepest thanks go to Diane Weber, my wife, for her unending support in this project and in so many others. I also want to thank her for suggesting that I work out my ideas on regulation in book form in the first place.

1. The Information Technology Revolution: A Brief History

Although this book analyzes the political and economic fallout from the information technology revolution, it does not pretend to be a book about technology. Still, some knowledge of the rapidly advancing capabilities of information technology is required to grasp the political and economic implications of recent developments. It is necessary to begin, therefore, with an overview of the fundamental advances in communications over the past several decades.

A Brief History of Microelectronics

The first shots in the information technology revolution were fired at AT&T's Bell Laboratories in the late 1940s.[1] When members of the Bell Labs' solid-state group demonstrated the transistor in 1947, they provided the key to the development of the microelectronics industry, including microprocessors, storage chips, and other integrated circuits that are the physical underpinnings of all information technology.

Before transistors, electronic machinery—whether a telephone exchange, a computer, or a television set—was large, unreliable, and had only limited capabilities. Most of the machinery made used the vacuum tube, a device invented in 1906 for switching and amplifying electrical signals. Although the vacuum tube was crucial to the development of television and radio communications, it suffered from serious performance limitations when used in more complex machinery such as telephone exchanges and computers.

---

[1] There is some irony in this, because the advances in information technology touched off by research at Bell Labs eventually destroyed AT&T's government-blessed monopoly over telephone communications in the United States. Clearly, the early information technology revolutionaries had no inkling that their research would lead ultimately to the breakup of the company that employed them.

1

Vacuum tubes are inherently unreliable. Even though individual tubes are unlikely to fail, when combined in large banks—as they were in early computers, for example—the probability rapidly increases that one of the vacuum tubes will fail, causing a system failure.[2] One possible solution is, of course, to build more reliable vacuum tubes, but that approach has its limits. The components of the tubes—wire, glass bulbs, metal rods, and so on—can prove faulty, working either individually or in combination. It was for that reason that the researchers at Bell Labs in the 1940s were looking for a new kind of electronic device to replace the vacuum tube. Their quest led them to develop a group of materials called semiconductors.

It was known in the 1940s that the addition of tiny amounts of impurities to semiconducting materials, which include the elements silicon and germanium, could change their electrical properties. Researchers at Bell Labs hoped to understand that process well enough to be able to deliberately "dope" semiconductors with impurities to create solid-state devices with the same amplification and switching capabilities as the vacuum tube. The result of their research was the transistor, first demonstrated on December 23, 1947.

Because transistors lack the complex structure of vacuum tubes, they are more reliable themselves and can therefore be used to build more reliable electronic equipment. In addition, transistors are smaller and lighter than vacuum tubes,[3] and they are less costly to produce.

So microelectronics was born. Transistors allowed scientists and engineers to imagine entire integrated circuits created in miniature on blocks of semiconducting material. Texas Instruments and Fairchild Semiconductor took over where Bell Labs left off, and today

---

[2]It is easy to see how this occurs. Suppose the probability of any one vacuum tube remaining functional during some extended period is very high, say 99 percent. If 100 such tubes are combined in some electronic computing or switching device, the probability of the entire collection of tubes remaining operational for the period in question can be found by multiplying 99 percent by itself 100 times. The result of that calculation is 37 percent. In other words, if you build a device using 100 electronic components, each of which is 99 percent reliable, you end up with a device that is only 37 percent reliable.

[3]The original transistor was about 100 times smaller than the standard vacuum tube of the time.

for throwaway prices millions of transistors and related devices can be built on a single chip of silicon a few millimeters square. These chips not only store information, they also process it.[4]

As important as the first integrated circuits were, they could carry out only a relatively limited number of functions. The next major breakthrough occurred in the early 1970s when the Intel Corporation developed the microprocessor, a general-purpose computer-on-a-chip. Like any general-purpose computer, microprocessors can be programmed and reprogrammed to carry out a wide variety of tasks, and they are becoming ever more powerful. The processing power of a computer can be measured in various ways, but it is generally acknowledged that the latest generation of personal computers using Intel's Pentium chip will be about 90 times as powerful as the original IBM personal computer.

Because microprocessors and other complex integrated circuits are now so cheap and so small, they have been incorporated into a wide range of electronic products. We now take for granted features and capabilities that were barely dreamed of a decade or so ago. In our living rooms are televisions capable of automatically fine-tuning station reception or adjusting the colors on the screen. Some televisions and VCRs can even freeze-frame images from live television broadcasts, and VCRs can be programmed to record a sitcom and then change channels and tape a movie. In our kitchens we have microwave ovens that can be programmed to optimally cook particular kinds of meat. Throughout our homes, we have installed telephones that can redial busy numbers or dial one of a repertory of frequently called numbers with the push of a button.

These advanced consumer devices are all children of the microelectronics revolution that began with the invention of the transistor. But microelectronics has had an even bigger impact at work. Readers familiar with offices as recently as the early 1980s will remember when they were full of dumb machines—typewriters, switchboards requiring a human operator, and copiers and fax machines that took up the space of two desks, were out of order much of the time, and produced poor quality output at the best of times. There were computers too. But they were huge beasts that

---

[4]For a brilliant history of microelectronics and its impact on communications and just about everything else, see George Gilder, *Microcosm* (New York: Simon and Schuster, 1989).

lurked in special rooms, needed their own air conditioning plants, and could be understood and programmed only by highly trained specialists.

By contrast, today's office equipment has microelectronic circuitry at its core. Typewriters evolved first into memory typewriters then into dedicated word processors. The word processors themselves were then replaced by general-purpose personal computers operating under instructions from word-processing software. Word-processing output is often produced by laser printers available for under $1,000. Less than a decade ago, such printers cost tens of thousands of dollars.

Microelectronics have also penetrated the office switchboard. Most switchboard functions are now carried out automatically, enabling individual employees to readily call outside the building or transfer a call to another desk. Today's telephone systems can carry computer data as well as voice calls, and they can store voice messages for later retrieval by users.

The microelectronics-led transformations are also apparent in the exchanges of the major telephone companies. Until the 1970s, telephone networks had only limited capabilities. Before microelectronics, public telephone exchanges were housed in huge buildings, and they were hard-pressed to reliably carry out the most basic switching functions—providing a dial tone, making a connection or transmitting a busy signal, and disconnecting at the end of the call. Over the past couple of decades, however, microelectronics has led not only to smaller, more reliable, and more cost-effective exchanges, but also to a wide range of new services. Thanks to the miracle of microelectronics, an intelligent telephone network, capable even of self-maintenance, is gradually emerging.

Many local telephone companies offer Caller-ID services, for example. The consumer or business with Caller ID can see the number of the calling party on a small liquid-crystal display before answering the telephone. Long-distance companies offer the same service under the name "Automatic Number Identification." Telemarketing firms and mail-order companies can use ANI to provide operators with information including the caller's name, address, credit information, and a list of previous orders. Some companies use ANI to automatically route an individual customer to an operator familiar with his account.

Another service now widely offered by telephone companies is voice mail. Callers can store messages on a computer disk drive for telephone subscribers who are away from their desks, out of the office, or just busy on other calls. Some long-distance companies are even adding enhanced voice-mail capabilities to their pay phone service. If a caller cannot reach his intended party, he can leave a taped message, and the telephone company will continue to attempt to forward the message at regular intervals until the message is delivered.

Other new telephone network capabilities are not quite as obvious. In long-distance communications, for example, services that once required special equipment and special telephone lines are now available without such investments. Thus toll-free (800) service, once the sole purview of large companies, is now available even to residential telephone subscribers who want to keep in touch with children at college or aged parents.

A complete list of communications services introduced over the past two decades would fill many pages. A list of the new services planned for the next decade would fill even more. But the novel equipment features and new services are not the most important part of the microelectronics story. Advancing technology is allowing engineers to pack more and more information-processing power into ever smaller spaces. That in turn has led to smaller, more powerful, and less expensive information-processing devices. It is not just telephone exchanges that are more intelligent; so are telephone handsets. Copiers and fax machines not only produce better quality products, but they are also now small enough to fit on a desktop. But the devolution of information-processing power brought about by microelectronics is most dramatically illustrated in the computing industry. In just over 10 years, personal computers (PCs) have gone from being little more than playthings for hobbyists to being the key computing resource for organizations of almost every size.

There are still big computers, of course. Indeed the corporate mainframe is a standard feature of most very large businesses. But there is a world of difference between the way large computers are used today and the way they were used in the past.

In the 1950s, when integrated circuitry was relatively primitive, corporate computing consisted of a centralized mainframe computer receiving its information from card readers or dumb terminals. In the 1960s, the ratio of price to performance in the microelectronic devices improved, and Digital Equipment Corporation, Data General Corporation, and several other companies introduced minicomputers. Minicomputers were still very large, powerful, and expensive machines, but companies could afford to put them in departments, allowing information handling to devolve from corporate headquarters to individual departments and regional offices. Despite such advances, however, from the 1950s through the 1970s, computers represented a major information bottleneck. The average employee handed over problems to the specially trained computer staff and then waited—hours, days, even weeks—for the results.

The 1980s saw a sea change. As circuitry became more densely packaged, increasingly powerful microprocessors were developed, and personal computers were introduced. PCs bring powerful information-handling capabilities to the desktop. Employees no longer need specialized technical knowledge to operate them. A few hours of training will suffice.

The PC has thus replaced the mainframe computer as the general-purpose computing workhorse. The corporate mainframe is now mainly the home of large databases too big to be stored on a single PC—customer and employee records and accounting information, for example. The corporate mainframe bottleneck has been eliminated, and the information flow through organizations is faster and more efficient than ever.

Personal computing has also led to the introduction of a new kind of network—the local area network. LANs can link together personal computers as well as connect them to departmental minicomputers and centralized mainframes. LAN users can exchange messages, call up files from other personal computers within the network, or access information from the larger computers. The LAN is also becoming the critical component of client/server or distributed computing. In client/server computing, different parts of an individual computing program may be stored on different machines, including not only personal computers but also larger machines. Running such programs requires the machines in the network to operate in harmony, but the end user of a client/server application effectively has access to a machine with the power of a supercomputer rather than just the PC in front of him. To use the phrase now current in the computing industry—with client/server, the network has become the computer.

The development of microelectronics and the consequent introduction of smaller, cheaper, more powerful, and more "featureful" information-processing devices have empowered individuals and small groups. Computing power has moved away from a technical elite and closer to the average citizen. Individuals and groups now have access to information-processing capabilities once available only to the largest organizations, if they were available at all. As the power to process and create information products has shifted from centralized bureaucracies to individuals, important new business opportunities have emerged throughout the economy.

I assume that such developments are in the public interest. I will contend throughout this book, however, that much government information policy tends to inhibit rather than promote the benefits of new technologies. And it is not just telephone and computer networks that are affected. The microelectronics revolution is leading to new service opportunities in the broadcasting and cable television industries, opportunities that could easily be delayed if not destroyed by improper or inadequate policy responses.

Shannon and the Theory of Information

Because of microelectronics, electronic intelligence is now found everywhere, and wherever electronic intelligence is found, information is stored, processed, and transmitted to other intelligent devices. But what exactly is information?

The man who effectively answered that question was mathematician Claude Shannon, one of the unsung heroes of the information technology revolution.[5] Two papers by Shannon on the theory of information revolutionized our understanding of the communications process and showed that all information, regardless of whether it appears as video, graphics, text, computer data, speech, or even genetic code, can be quantified in the same manner.[6]

---

[5]Shannon was employed by Bell Labs at the time of his path-breaking work on information technology.

[6]See Claude Shannon, "The Mathematical Theory of Communication," *Bell System Technical Journal* 27 (1948): 379–423 and 623–56. Building on Shannon's work, the maverick computer scientist, Edward Fredkin, has theorized that the basic stuff of the universe is neither the classical waves and particles of Newtonian physics nor the ephemeral particle-waves of quantum theory, but rather pure information. For more on the work of Fredkin, see Robert Wright, *Three Scientists and Their Gods* (New York: Times Books, 1988), pp. 3–80.

When Shannon was developing information theory in the late 1940s, he was concerned with the limits of information transmission over a "noisy" channel. His theory demonstrated that as long as an information source puts out information at a rate that does not swamp the capacity of the channel over which it is being transmitted, it is always possible to encode the information in such a way that it can be understood at the other end of the channel, no matter how noisy the channel. Profound as Shannon's results are, they are less important than the fact that to prove them, he came up with the first precise scientific measure and definition of information.

Shannon conceived of information as something that removes uncertainty about an event. A weather forecast provides information in Shannon's sense if after listening to it, we are more certain than before about whether it is going to rain. On the other hand, if we can look out the window and see that it is raining hard, a weather report that tells us it is going to rain conveys no information, according to Shannon.

Shannon's theory of information involves much mathematical abstraction, as is inevitable for a theory that encompasses everything from weather forecasts to the information contained in a picture hanging in an art gallery. It is not necessary, however, to discuss his work in detail to understand how he defined the basic atom of information—the bit. Bits are as fundamental to the Information Age as Newtonian forces were to the age of the machine.

Shannon defined a bit in terms of an "either-or" situation in which a piece of information reduces our uncertainty to zero. All information can be thought of as consisting of a certain number of bits. One way of conceptualizing this is in terms of the maximum number of yes-no questions that must be answered to extract the desired information from a person or a machine.

Suppose, for example, that you are interested in buying a set of dishes. You know the dishes are available in pink and in blue, and you know that the store near you has only one set. This is the either-or situation: The set of dishes at the store is either pink or it is blue, although you do not know which. To determine the color of the available dishes, all you have to do is ask whether the dishes in the warehouse are blue. If the answer is yes, you know the dishes are blue. If the answer is no, you know the dishes are pink. Either way, the answer to your question contains one bit of information because only one question was needed to elicit the desired information.

Suppose now that our hypothetical dishes come in four colors— blue, pink, green, and gold. In such a case, you may have to ask up to three yes-no questions to determine the color of the dishes in the warehouse. In the first example, the statement "The dishes in the warehouse are pink" contained one bit of information. In this second case, it contains three bits of information.

The principles of quantifying information in terms of bits can be generalized to much more complex situations than the color of dishes. But bits are a static measure. In communications we are concerned with the amount of information that can be transmitted in a given period of time. Hence, the fundamental measure here is not bits, but rather bits per second (bps).[7]

Shannon's theory thus conceives of information flows as streams of discrete bits. This kind of information is typified by the 1s and 0s that travel between computers when they talk to each other. Information consisting of discrete bits is called "digital information." The other kind of information is "analog information." Analog information is continuously varying. Human speech, for example, is intrinsically analog because it is not naturally divided into a finite number of frequencies.

Analog information can be converted into digital information by sampling it at discrete intervals and coding each sample in digital form. If the sampling intervals are sufficiently short, any information lost in the process of analog-to-digital conversion will be insignificant. Because analog information can be converted into digital form, Shannon's theory of information can be applied to all forms of information. From a practical perspective, that means that speech or pictures, intrinsically analog information, can be converted into and transmitted as digital information.

---

[7]Typically in telecommunications we talk about kilobits per second (kbps, thousands of bits per second) or megabits per second (Mbps, millions of bits per second). Occasionally, we talk about gigabits per second (Gbps, billions of bits per second). To get a feel for what these terms mean, consider that most personal computer modems run at 2.4 kbps or 9.6 kbps; local area networks that link together many PCs in a building operate at between 1 Mbps and 100 Mbps; and a very busy telephone network trunk line may operate at 2.4 Gbps.

All modern PBXs and telephone company exchanges transmit speech in digitized form, for example.[8] Videoconferencing, a corporate communications tool of growing importance, is based on the digitization of analog video signals. In fact there has been a digital revolution that parallels the microelectronics revolution discussed earlier.[9]

Digital information, expressed as it is in streams of 1s and 0s or yeses and noes, is much easier for a machine to process and recognize than analog information with its infinite collection of frequencies. Compare an old-fashioned analog telephone communications link with a modern digital telephone link, for example. In both cases the information may be transmitted over the same kind of electrical communications link. In both cases, the signal carrying the information is subject to the same types of electrical and magnetic interference. But here the similarity between analog and digital communications ends, and the difference shows up at the far end of the link, where the receiver must interpret the signal.

In analog communications the receiver typically makes no adjustments for distortions, and even small distortions can become noticeable interference by the time the message has been sent through an extensive network from one transceiver to another. Distortions may accumulate to a point where the message is unintelligible.

In digital communications, all the receiver must do is recognize whether each bit of information coming its way is a 1 or a 0. Digital receivers are designed to count any electrical blip within a certain frequency range as a 1 and any blip within another frequency range as a 0. When electromagnetic disturbances knock the reading slightly off the exact value for a 1 or a 0, messages are still interpreted correctly, and the signal is effectively regenerated before being passed on to another node in the network.

---

[8] A PBX is a private branch exchange, the term commonly used in the telephone industry for an office telephone switchboard and the system supporting it.

[9] There is nothing really new about digital communications, however. Telegraph operators using Morse code were communicating in digital form. Because we are now returning to digital communications after more than a century, the analog telephone network has been referred to by one commentator as "a 100-year mistake." See Leonard Kleinrock, "High Speed Networks," Paper presented at a workshop, Networks for the Coming Information Age, held in Fairfax, Virginia, 1989, sponsored by George Mason University and the Institute of Electrical and Electronic Engineers, Washington and Northern Virginia sections.

Digital communications thus produce fewer errors. That is relatively unimportant in voice communications, but accuracy is vital in data communications. (Imagine the 1s and 0s in the link represent funds being transferred electronically.) Since errors are less of a problem, digital links can also often transfer information more quickly than analog links can. Digital microelectronic circuitry is also easier and cheaper to produce than its analog equivalent.

One of the fundamental assumptions of U.S. telecommunications policy has been that print-based publishers of information and companies that broadcast information electronically should be subject to different regulatory and legal treatment because the information provided in the different contexts is somehow inherently different. As we shall see, the combination of microelectronics and digitization is making the validity of this argument increasingly less apparent.

The Quest for Bandwidth

Bandwidth is the measure of the capacity of a communications channel. The bigger the bandwidth, the more information—that is, the more bits—you can send down the channel.[10] The bandwidth of a channel stretching from 300 kHz to 310 kHz is 10 kHz, for example, and such a channel would have 10 times the capacity of a channel with a lower bound of 500 kHz and an upper bound of 501 kHz. In other words, the 10-kHz channel could carry 10 times the amount of information that the 1-kHz channel could in the same amount of time. Although strictly speaking the bandwidth of a communications channel should be measured in terms of frequency, the "bandwidth" of a digital channel is more often given in terms of the speed with which it carries information—that is, in terms of bits per second.

One way to view the history of electronic communications is as a quest for more bandwidth. The telegraph did not need very high bandwidths. Telephones needed somewhat more bandwidth than telegraph communications. Television required higher bandwidths than either telephone or telegraph, and if high-definition digital

---

[10]Technically, bandwidth has nothing to do with bits. It is really an analog measure. In fact, it is just the difference between the upper and lower frequencies of the electromagnetic wave carried by a communications channel, but that statistic also turns out to be a measure of the information-carrying capacity of the channel.

television ever becomes a reality, it will be particularly hungry for bandwidth.

Since channels with high bandwidth must, by definition, travel over media capable of supporting high frequencies, engineers and inventors have spent the past 100 years looking for new transmission technologies. Iron wires that carried telegraph messages could not support the frequencies necessary to carry long-distance telephone calls without severe distortions. So telephone companies moved to copper wire pairs. That worked well (and continues to work well) in much of the telephone network, but by the 1950s the routes between major telephone exchanges had become so busy that they needed more bandwidth than regular copper wire pairs could carry. The telephone companies therefore started to use coaxial cable. Video is a huge consumer of bandwidth, so when the cable-television industry began to emerge in the 1960s it too used coaxial cable for its networks. Atmospheric communications saw a similar evolution, from the relatively low frequencies used for conventional radio to the much higher frequency microwaves used in satellite communications and in some long-distance telephone networks.

The digital revolution made the quest for bandwidth all the more urgent. When intrinsically analog information is converted into digital form, it requires much higher bandwidths than it does in analog mode. High-quality digital video communications can easily require channels with bandwidths running into tens of megabits per second, for example. Coaxial cable can support two to three digital video channels over extended distances, but using analog signals, cable television companies are able to transmit 80 or more channels over their coaxial systems.

Telecommunications engineers have known for some time that very high bandwidths would be available by using some form of optical communications—that is, communications using light rather than radio waves or microwaves.[11] Communications using visible light offer bandwidths about 10 million times greater than

[11]Light, radio waves, and microwaves are all forms of electromagnetic radiation. They differ only in their frequency, but this also means that they differ in their information-carrying capacity.

microwave communications.[12] But there are problems. Over-the-air optical communications are possible only over very short distances for the obvious reason that over extended distances, things like clouds and flocks of birds tend to get in the way. For optical communications to be a practical possibility, then, some kind of "pipe" had to be developed through which optical signals could be sent free of obstruction. Such light pipes were first constructed from rigid straight-line segments and a series of mirrors, but that proved as unworkable as it sounds. Expensive civil engineering work was required, and even slight earth vibrations could throw the link off kilter.

The solution to the light pipe problem was eventually found in the use of fiber optics in which the light runs down a flexible glass fiber. Such fiber was first constructed in the 1950s, but it was not until the mid-1960s that two researchers from Standard Telephone Laboratories in the United Kingdom showed that it was possible to transmit information at optical frequencies over several hundred feet of fiber if the glass was pure enough. Fiber-optic links are driven by tiny semiconductor lasers and light-emitting diodes, both products of the microelectronics revolution.[13]

Fiber optics was initially used only for connecting telephone exchanges in busy downtown areas of major cities. As optical communications technology improved, fiber started to penetrate long-distance networks. More recently, telephone companies have started deploying fiber in the local loop, the segment of the telephone network between the local telephone exchange and customers' premises. In a few cases telephone companies have actually brought fiber all the way into homes and are providing both voice and video entertainment services over the same fiber equipment. Unfortunately, government regulation is currently frustrating the local telephone companies' attempts to provide more advanced services over fiber.

The microelectronics and digital revolutions may now be entering a sprightly middle age, but the optical revolution has barely begun.

---

[12]Microwave communications underpinned much of long-distance telephony until recently, and it is still important for satellite communications.

[13]Purists will note that fiber optics does not use visible light, but rather infrared light with frequencies slightly below those of visible light.

Optical fiber will increasingly be used in every kind of communications network. Many new commercial buildings are being wired with optical fiber as they are built. Fiber will thus provide the physical underpinning for the high-speed computer networks that will eventually serve the occupants of those buildings. Fiber can also be found within telephone exchanges, connecting circuit boards and improving the performance of the public telephone networks.

That is just the beginning. Although fiber optics represented a huge improvement over earlier forms of transmission technology, it is still relatively inefficient. Practical fiber-optic links allow information transmission at rates well below the theoretical limits of optical communications because to some extent today's fiber optics is still a hybrid affair. Light is pulsed down a glass fiber, but the pulsing is done with electricity. Completely optical transmission is on its way, and it will lead to huge increases in the information-carrying capacity of communications networks. In the near future better light sources and detectors and fiber made of specialized forms of glass are expected to increase transmission rates by factors of up to 1,000. Optical switching chips will speed up both computers and (what is really the same thing) communications equipment. Over the next 50 years, current electronic communications networks will gradually give way to a wholly optical network in which fiber optics links together ultrafast optical switches and optical storage devices that will dwarf today's magnetic disk and tape drives in capacity. When that happens we will have truly entered the Information Age.

Bandwidth Counterrevolutions

If fiber optics is revolutionizing the ability of networks to carry information, two important counterrevolutionary developments are also on the horizon that will make fiber optics a less important stride forward than it would have been otherwise. New technologies are being developed that will increase the information-carrying capacity of networks without using fiber.

The first of these developments is digital compression, which relies on the fact that any image or sequence of images (which is all that video is) contains a considerable amount of information that is redundant because it remains unchanged and is repeated in several frames.[14] By eliminating the redundancy, compression reduces the amount of data that has to be transmitted. Digital video and image transmissions that would barely fit into a fiber-optic trunk in their raw form can, as a result of compression, be run over traditional copper cable networks.

Compression is used in a variety of ways. It allows facsimile transmissions and video teleconferencing to take place over normal telephone wires, both of which would require fiber-optic networks in its absence. Cable television companies are planning to use it to expand the capacity of their coaxial cable–based networks from 80 channels to several hundred channels. It also underpins most serious attempts to bring high-definition television into the home. Without compression, HDTV transmissions require fiber-optic networks, and although by the middle of the next century most homes will probably have fiber coming all the way to the telephone jack, installing all that fiber will be a lengthy and expensive process. At present, no more than a few hundred homes have fiber installed—and those installations have all been experimental rather than commercial.

There has also been a second counterrevolutionary development as engineers have sought ways to use existing transmission networks more efficiently. Improvements in transmission equipment, due again to microelectronics, have meant that copper cable can carry much higher bandwidths than previously thought possible, albeit for short distances. Those improvements open the way for hybrid networks that use fiber optics to transport information at high rates over extended distances to local hubs and then use coaxial cable or telephone wires to transport the information to individual end users. Such an approach reduces considerably the cost of delivering high-capacity communications to end users because copper-based communications are much less expensive than fiber optics.[15] There is a growing consensus that really high-capacity residential communications will come first, not in the form of "fiber-to-the-home," but rather as "fiber-to-the-curb." Fiber-to-the-curb would thus use fiber to bring television and other forms of information to a hub serving several homes. Twisted-pair telephone

[14]Consider the background against which the main action in a movie is shot, for example.

[15]This is not just because copper cable is less expensive than optical cable. The main factor is the cost of the optical transmitters, receivers, and cable connectors.

15

wires would then carry the signals to individual residences. A similar approach is being tried in the computer world, where wide-area data networks using fiber are being connected to copper for local connection to powerful computer workstations.

Many policymakers seem largely unaware of these counterrevolutionary trends conserving bandwidth and using existing transmission networks more efficiently. Most denizens of Washington apparently believe that the only way to develop the communications infrastructure is to encourage telephone companies to install as much fiber as possible. The general ignorance of technological developments displayed by those who regulate the telecommunications industry is appalling. It also indicates why one cannot expect too much from the government when it comes to a successful industrial policy for the telecommunications industry.

Convergence

It is obvious to even casual observers that the developments of microelectronics, digitization, and high-speed transmission networks have had a profound impact on the ways in which we receive and use information. From a policy perspective, one of the most important repercussions has occurred because of convergence.

Telecommunications policy has long been based on the premise that information transmitted over wires could be easily distinguished from information transmitted over the air. Different rules and regulations were written for different information media. Over the past 40 to 50 years, however, information has become increasingly fluid, and what was once obvious about the ways in which particular types of information were stored and transmitted is no longer so apparent.

The consequences of digitization can be seen (or rather, heard) in the enormous improvement over the past couple of decades in the voice quality of long-distance telephone calls and in the super-high fidelity we now expect from compact discs. But the digital revolution has done much more than just provide improved signal quality. The simple binary form of digital information also makes such information easy to manipulate and transform from one format to another. There are now devices, for example, that can take text stored in a digital form and transform it into audible speech. With the appropriate equipment you can call your computer for your electronic mail, and a machine will read it to you.

This fluidity of information format is also reflected in information storage. Once it is digitized, voice, video, text, and data are all much the same. Thus compact discs, most familiar to the general public as a means of playing recorded music, are being used increasingly to store computer data and even video. As a result of the digitization of information and the ability to store a page of Shakespeare and a music video from Michael Jackson on the same medium, new forms of multimedia communications are emerging in which text, voice, and image communications are combined in a single interactive, user-friendly format.

It is this fluidity of information formats that constitutes convergence. Convergence has resulted from both the recognition that all information can be converted into the same binary digital form and the development of microelectronics that makes such a conversion possible while providing the means for conveniently and economically manipulating digital information. Convergence is not only central to the Information Age, it affects every level of information technology—hardware, software, and services.

As cheap multifunctional circuitry is incorporated into everything from large computers to consumer electronics, convergence is most noticeable at the hardware level. There are numerous examples: equipment that doubles as an optical storage device for personal computers and also plays compact discs, devices that serve as both telephone and computer terminals, television sets that provide access to interactive consumer information services, "black boxes" that combine functions that were once carried out by several pieces of data communications equipment, and so on. Networks are also beginning to overlap: PBXs now serve as the hubs of computer networks, or they can call up relevant information from large host computers while processing a call. Telephone networks transmit video images, and personal computer networks handle telephone calls.

That is where fiber optics comes in. Increasing convergence will mean a growing demand for bandwidth. Eventually only the huge capabilities of fiber optics will be able to meet that demand. The new multimedia services born of convergence, especially those incorporating video, will be much more bandwidth-hungry than most currently available services. Fiber optics will bring those services into our homes, offices, and factories. And as the number of networks serving multiple purposes increases, there will be an increasing need to link networks together with high-bandwidth trunking. Again, fiber optics will be the ideal medium to supply the trunking. Finally, electronic connections for business communications, personal interactions, and entertainment will continue to grow in volume, straining existing networks to capacity. More bandwidth will be needed, bandwidth fiber optics can provide. Thus convergence, a trend born of the microelectronic and digital revolutions, will be brought to fruition by the optical communications revolution.

Convergence is shattering the boundaries that have defined the information-related industries for a century or more. Telephone companies are being pulled into publishing and broadcasting, and cable television companies are finding new opportunities in the data communications business. Regulators and regulations are not well suited for dealing with such dramatic change. But more about that in the next chapter.

2. Telecommunications Regulation and the Three-Segment Model

Government intervention in electronic communications markets has been justified in several ways. Much communications regulation is based on the notion that the public owns the airwaves. Accordingly the government must oversee and regulate their use, guided by principles of fairness and efforts to ensure outlets for diverse viewpoints. Many communications companies are also viewed as monopolies—natural or otherwise—and so in need of government oversight. Interestingly, policymakers rarely encourage competition for those monopolies, preferring instead to protect consumers by imposing rate and service regulations.

These two traditional arguments for government oversight are being undermined by the convergence phenomenon discussed in chapter 1. Advocates of regulation are therefore promoting new justifications, including industrial policy and national security. The most visible manifestation of the recent trend is the fuss over high-definition television and national computing networks.

When the industrial-policy approach to telecommunications regulation fails, as it surely will, new justifications will be sought. Policymakers will not easily give up control over an industry as important as telecommunications. It is important, therefore, to demonstrate that current trends in communications technology have done more than just make obsolete a particular reason for regulation or a particular type of regulation. Recent developments have made regulation itself obsolete. It is my purpose in this chapter to begin to make that case.

One could approach the task by pointing to the contrast between the ever accelerating speed with which information technology is developing and the lack of speed with which regulators adapt regulations. Regulators are not keeping up, and their lagging behind is leading to inevitable arbitrariness and misjudgments. Though telling, this argument cannot by itself deliver a killing blow to the persistent doctrine that the government must play a central role in electronic communications.

In the first place, those who believe in the need for regulation might simply respond that the pace of change should be slowed by artificial means. In the second place, communications technology is not changing quite as quickly as popular accounts might lead one to believe. It often takes from two to five years for a new telecommunications technology to travel from the laboratory to the marketplace, and another five years may elapse before the technology is widely deployed. Theoretically, at least, regulators could put in place procedures that would allow them to adapt to such a pace of change.

As noted in chapter 1, however, changes in the telecommunications industry go much deeper than a mere increased pace of technological change. Convergence is changing fundamentally the way we think about information and communications services. Thus convergence is the ultimate nemesis of telecommunications regulation, for in the face of telecommunications convergence, regulators quite literally no longer know what they are talking about! In this setting, legal and regulatory limits are rapidly becoming overly strict, largely inapplicable, and generally destructive.

Telecommunications Regulation: The Three-Segment Model

Traditionally, communications regulators and policymakers have based their decisions on the three-segment model. The communications industry has long been viewed as being naturally divided into three segments: common carriers, the print media, and broadcasters. Each segment of the industry has its own regulatory regime, and state and federal regulators as well as the courts have based their rulings on the acceptance of these three distinct subindustries.

Common carriers include telephone companies, telegraph companies, electronic-mail companies, public-data networks, and the postal service. All provide a means of transporting information; they do not provide the information itself. When common carriers are regulated, the regulatory regime that generally governs is one of fair and nondiscriminatory access. At the heart of regulation of the telephone industry, for example, is the concept of universal service. Both state and federal policies are presumably designed so that basic telephone service is affordable to almost anyone. As a further consequence of their common-carrier status, telephone companies generally cannot refuse to serve homes and businesses located within their service area. A similar philosophy is behind government policies affecting the postal system.

Newspapers, magazines, and book publishers represent the second communications segment, the print media. For print media, the primary regulatory paradigm is the freedom of the press as guaranteed in the First Amendment to the Constitution.[1] This amendment has clearly occupied a preferred position in the hierarchy of constitutional rights and powers for many years.

Given the importance the Supreme Court has attached to the First Amendment's protection of freedom of the press, it is somewhat surprising that the broadcasting industry has not enjoyed similar protection by the First Amendment's guarantee of free speech. Broadcasting, the third of the communications subindustries, has its own regime, strongly influenced by the presumed public ownership of the airwaves. The government (primarily through the Federal Communications Commission) plays the role of public trustee, with the right to allocate broadcasting capacity and control its use in the public interest.

Regulators have traditionally used two methods to control broadcast capacity, or more specifically the type of information being broadcast. First, regulators claim the right to determine what radio and television broadcasters may, may not, and must broadcast. Traditionally, that claim has included both the right to control offensive language in broadcast programming and, through application of the Fairness Doctrine, the right to insist on balanced coverage of controversial issues.[2]

---

[1]The First Amendment reads, "Congress shall make no law respecting an establishment of religion, or prohibiting the free exercise thereof; or abridging the freedom of speech, or of the press; or the right of the people peaceably to assemble, and to petition the Government for a redress of grievances." The Supreme Court has never interpreted the First Amendment as a rule without limits, of course. The government can, for example, force print media to compensate victims of defamation.

[2]The FCC repealed the Fairness Doctrine in 1987, and the commission has substantially reduced its direct efforts to ensure balanced coverage on controversial issues. The FCC continues its efforts to control offensive language in radio and television broadcasts, however, as in the regulatory condemnation of radio personality Howard Stern in the fall of 1992. The FCC fined the radio station that carried his show on the grounds that it was obscene.

Regulators have also attempted to influence broadcast content by determining who owns broadcast stations. Ownership rules have evolved over the years, but they continue to include limits on the number of stations a person or company can own in one market, limits on the extent to which other media companies (most notably newspapers) can own broadcast stations, and regulations designed to favor minority ownership of broadcast stations.[3] Although never a formal part of the Fairness Doctrine, station-ownership control and the Fairness Doctrine are closely related philosophically. Both assume that the public interest is served when the government promotes diversity of broadcast program content. Station-ownership control is supposed to ensure diversity by ensuring that no single individual or group is in a position to dominate programming decisions on a large number of stations.[4]

Despite some apparent inconsistencies, the three-segment model has at least been easy to apply. If the communications medium is a newspaper, then apply the First Amendment. If it is a telephone company, then FCC regulation will aim primarily at assuring universal, nondiscriminatory access. In regulating broadcasters, the FCC focuses on fairness in both content and the allocation of broadcasting licenses. Unfortunately for regulators, it is becoming ever more difficult to neatly categorize communications companies, and determining which regulatory paradigm to apply will only become more ambiguous as the Information Age unfolds.

Convergence and Regulation

The growing recognition that words and pictures, in printed, audio, and video forms, can be digitized and transmitted over or stored on a wide range of media is blurring the lines between the

---

[3]Broadcast licensees are also subject to the 12-18-18 rule. That is, licensees are limited to owning a maximum of 12 television stations, 18 AM radio stations, and 18 FM radio stations nationwide.

[4]Imagine such rules' being applied to the publishing industry. Suppose that regulations required all published material to offer a fair and balanced discussion of controversial issues, or imagine a government panel allocating licenses determining who could and could not publish a newspaper. Such laws would never survive the scrutiny of a constitutional court. With broadcasting, however, public interest considerations apparently warrant just such meddling.

three traditional segments of the communications industry.[5] It is becoming ever more difficult for regulators to determine what regulatory regime to apply to communications companies with characteristics of all three segments of the communications industry. The widespread consensus that once marked regulatory and legislative communications policy prescriptions no longer exists. Recent court battles waged over the role of the regional Bell operating companies in providing information services (i.e., electronic publishing) demonstrate deep differences of opinion among judges, and lawmakers are tempted to second-guess court decisions when they are handed down. Similar battles can be expected over the FCC's recent decision to allow the telephone companies to enter the cable-television business (i.e., broadcasting). Things will only get worse.

Examples of the convergence of the segments of the communications industry abound, but its consequences can be demonstrated more easily if we concentrate on the evolving role of one segment. Let us consider the future of publishing. Although any look into the future is marked by uncertainty, the technology in my scenario already exists, and I believe the demand exists for the services I will describe. Regulators may slow the pace at which this scenario unfolds, but they are unlikely to keep it in check forever.

Newspapers Today

Newspaper technology is currently a strange hybrid of the ancient and the modern. Modern technology is apparent in the writing and editing of news stories. Reporters have access to computerized databases and media satellites from which to gather news. Stories are written on desktop or laptop computer terminals, and proofreading marks are entered as the stories are written. Reporters' computers are linked to a computerized typesetting system, which then feeds its data to the printing presses. If a story is prepared wholly from information stored on an electronic database, as is the case with some obituaries, the whole journalistic

---

[5]Telephone companies are capable of entering both the publishing and the broadcasting businesses, for example, and they are eager to do so. They have thus far been largely prevented from expanding into other communications businesses, however, because of the fear that they will abuse their supposed monopoly power. The legal status of the telephone companies will be discussed more thoroughly in the next chapter.

process—from information gathering to the output of the actual newspaper—can be carried out in digital electronic mode.

But here we leave the realm of high-tech. Once the information (the news) is gathered and processed by reporters, newspapers deliver that information much as they did 100 years ago. First the news stories are printed on paper. Then the papers are delivered to individual homes and offices and to the newsstands. The end product can be daunting. The *New York Times* for Friday, November 13, 1987, was 1,612 pages long and weighed 12 pounds.[6] It would seem that the newspaper industry could come up with a more user-friendly form of delivery.

If the news is gathered and processed in digital form, why not distribute it in digital form, too? The information could be delivered directly to computer terminals and workstations in homes and offices. The number of hard copies printed could be drastically reduced, resulting in dramatic savings in labor costs. Because computers are uniquely capable of searching through vast quantities of data for specific items, consumers would be better able to pick and choose stories of interest. Computer communications also allow for two-way transactions, implying that computer delivery of the news could be combined with an electronic message service as well as home shopping and banking services. This amalgam of services is generally known as "videotex."

A Future for Videotex?

Prodigy, a service launched jointly by IBM and Sears, is a form of videotex. It is still too early to predict the long-term future of Prodigy, but generally speaking, videotex has not been a success in the United States. In mid-1992, it was reported that IBM and Sears had invested $1 billion in Prodigy, and the service was still a long way from breaking even.[7]

The newspaper industry has also experimented with videotex. Times Mirror and Knight-Ridder were both actively involved in the development of videotex in the early 1980s. To date, however,

---

[6]Richard Saul Wurman, *Information Anxiety* (New York: Bantam, 1990), p. 33.

[7]"IBM and Sears Continue to Throw Money at Prodigy," *Computergram International*, no. 1928 (May 25, 1992). If the combined marketing force of IBM and Sears cannot make this medium work, one must wonder about the validity of the fundamental concept.

videotex projects in the United States have had average life spans of only about two years, and all have lost money.

The thing nearest to videotex that has enjoyed any commercial success is on-line information utilities, the best known of which is CompuServe. These utilities have many of the features of true consumer videotex, but most of what the user sees on his screen is in text form, while true videotex would include graphics. (At this point, the "video" in videotex is mere wishful thinking.) These information utilities are also targeted more toward computer enthusiasts than the general public, and their emphasis is on providing a means of exchange between like-minded people. CompuServe, for example, includes many "special interest groups" covering everything from literature and religion to specialized topics in computer science. General news and consumer services tend to take a back seat.

There are, of course, computer-based on-line services that emphasize news coverage. But they are aimed at people who have a business reason for wanting to access the information. There are a number of such services, including Vu/Text, a service recently acquired by Dialog from Knight-Ridder that offers the full text of some 80 U.S. newspapers, more than 200 business journals, numerous magazines and newswires, and international sources. The many on-line financial news services also fall into this category. There is nothing really new in this, of course. Electronic delivery of news for use by professional journalists is as old as the wire service.

Recent trends have been anything but encouraging, but it may not be necessary to give up on consumer videotex forever. Several problems must be addressed before newspapers can send the digital information they compile and store directly to homes and offices. One problem is price. On-line services have traditionally been expensive, and their pricing structures have been complex. Such attributes are a sure turnoff for potential consumer subscribers.

An even more important barrier is the sparsity of terminal equipment capable of receiving videotex.[8] Although some videotex companies have tried to market their own specialized terminals, those

---

[8]France is the only country where videotex has enjoyed significant success. There the government embarked on a program in the early 1980s to give away computer terminals for home use.

terminals can often do no more than access that company's service. The best hope for home videotex lies in home computers that can serve as videotex terminals among their other uses. Over the past decade, however, many frustrated home-computer users have discovered that once the novelty wore off, they could find nothing useful to do with their PCs. After an initial burst, the home-computer business has become the slowest growing segment of the PC market. Approximately 25 percent of American homes now contain PCs, but no more than 30 percent of them have the modems necessary to access videotex.

Still, there are many reasons to expect that the penetration of American homes by PCs will accelerate over the next decade. For one thing, prices will continue to decline for ever more powerful home computers. As computers are able to do more things, and do them faster and more effectively, they will become more attractive purchases. And unlike some of the early machines that were difficult to use or required specialized knowledge, home computers and their sophisticated programs are becoming ever more accessible, even to persons without formal computer training.

In addition, as young people who have never known a world without computers establish their own households, they will be inclined to install computers in their homes with the same kind of nonchalance with which an earlier generation bought television sets. Indeed, the dawn of the HDTV era will add further impetus to the home computing momentum.[9] The insides of high-definition televisions will look much like home computers, and they will undoubtedly include communications interfaces capable of hooking into videotex services.[10]

---

[9]I am somewhat skeptical of some of the claims currently made for HDTV, but there is little doubt that there will be a trend toward advanced television systems in the next decade.

[10]The cost of adding such interfaces to televisions will become increasingly trivial. That has been the history of the interfaces. In the mid-1980s, the modems used by most PCs in homes and small businesses operated at 0.3 kbps and cost $100 to $200. Modems operating at 9.6 kbps were considered state-of-the-art and cost thousands of dollars. After dropping in price to $30 or so, the old 0.3 kbps modems have now disappeared from the market. Meanwhile, 9.6 kbps are now quite common and cost $200 to $300.

Home computers appearing by the end of the century will finally be able to fulfill the dreams of the early creators of the microcomputer, serving individuals and families as entertainment centers, calculators, communications devices, text processors, home-control centers, security devices, and videotex terminals. And when home computers are able to provide that multitude of services, the cost associated with providing any one service will be small. Thus, the marginal cost of obtaining the capability to hook into videotex will be minimal and the audience for videotex will begin to expand.

Once a critical mass is reached, videotex providers will be able to pay for their services through a combination of advertising revenue and low user fees—just like today's newspapers.[11] The critical point will probably be reached sometime in the first decade of the next century, and when it arrives, low-cost widespread videotex will sound the death knell for the newspaper industry as a producer of paper products. With terminals commonplace in homes and offices, physical distribution will not survive. The newspaper industry will undoubtedly endure, but it will have to change. It will become one of the many information providers feeding a burgeoning, interconnected worldwide information network.

As the newspaper industry evolves, regulators will face the question of what regulatory regime to apply to this reformed provider of electronic information. The industry itself will, no doubt, expect to be granted the same First Amendment rights it has always received. But consider for a moment what an Information-Age newspaper company will look like.

On the newsroom floor, journalists and editors will create an electronic database of news. They will distribute the news to millions of electronic terminals in homes and offices throughout the country. This process should sound familiar; in another context it is called "broadcasting." Broadcast journalists also collect information, turn it into electronic form, and distribute it through terminals (radios or TVs) to end users. Over the next 10 to 20 years the convergence phenomenon will make it virtually impossible to make concrete distinctions between the newspaper industry, which is

[11]The notion of a critical mass is not unique to videotex, of course. It was necessary that a certain number of households own VCRs before movie rental businesses made sense. Obviously, the advent of movie rental stores also made owning a VCR more attractive.

protected by the First Amendment, and the broadcast industry, which is not.

Some observers will presumably then argue that the newspaper industry should be regulated like the broadcast industry. If such arguments hold sway, the FCC would gain at least some control over the content of the information newspapers publish as well as control over the number of newspaper companies any single entity could own. Such regulations have no parallel in today's newspaper business.

Policymakers may attempt to avoid such problems by establishing definitions designed to preserve the traditional distinctions between broadcasting and the press. But such attempts are bound to be arbitrary and doomed to failure. Suppose, for example, that some regulator, judge, or lawmaker tries to capitalize on the fact that broadcast journalists have traditionally used sound and (in the case of television) moving pictures, while newspaper journalists have generally used text. When distributed over videotex networks in the convergent information environment of the future, newspapers may well include sound, text, still images, and video. Distinguishing between such a newspaper and traditional broadcasting will be a hopeless task. Efforts to establish meaningful regulatory categories on the basis of interactive vs. noninteractive services are likely to prove equally futile as both broadcast and published information will become increasingly interactive as the Information Age unfolds.

Newspapers are not the only part of the publishing industry that will move toward electronic delivery. Some of the publishing industry has already taken steps in that direction. That could mean that the FCC will become the overlord of the publishing industry, or it could mean that broadcasting will get First Amendment protection.

Publishing the Telephone Directory

Complicating matters further is the evolving role of the common carriers—especially the telephone companies. As common carriers, telephone companies have been expected to provide fair and open access to all who want to use their networks. The proscriptions against telephone companies' supplying information has been one method used by regulators to ensure that all telephone customers are treated equally. As long as telephone companies transport only information, they are in no way threatened by or competing with those firms that supply the information.

Until recently, telephone companies were content to be common carriers. They had neither the ambition nor the technology to provide information directly—with one small exception. In publishing the telephone directory, telephone companies provide information. But that function is so closely tied to providing telephone service that it would seem foolish to exclude them from it. Besides, allowing telephone companies to publish telephone directories seemed safe enough as long as publishing remained in a pre–Information Age state.

As we enter the Information Age, however, the business of publishing telephone directories is moving from hard copy to on-line delivery, just as with many other publishing businesses. Nationwide on-line versions of both the yellow pages and the white pages are already available in the United States on a limited basis. In France, on-line white pages are widely available, although only because the national telecommunications monopoly has been distributing the necessary terminals without charge.[12]

Directories are particularly suited to electronic publishing. Hard-copy directories are bulky, difficult to use, and hard to update. Replacing them with an electronic database accessed through home terminals or personal computers would eliminate most of these problems while granting users access to a national directory rather than just to local ones.

Like all on-line information services, however, electronic directories have much in common with broadcasts. That quality has led Judge Harold Greene to argue that telephone companies, as common carriers, should not be allowed to offer such services.[13] In

[12]Various policy studies have called for a similar program in the United States. Many U.S. policymakers are apparently convinced that the French Minitel videotex service has no counterpart in this country. There are, however, hundreds of thousands of individual subscribers to the CompuServe Information Service, and they have access to a low-cost national on-line white pages. For more money, a personal-computer owner can access the Dialog information service, which includes a national yellow pages database.

[13]Harold Greene is the federal judge who oversees the Modification of Final Judgment (MFJ), the agreement that in 1982 settled the antitrust case between the U.S. government and AT&T. Since the antitrust case ended, this agreement (and its ongoing interpretation by Judge Greene) has formed one of the foundations on which the regulation of AT&T and the Bell companies is based. Judge Greene is

1987, when he reviewed the original ban preventing the Baby Bells from supplying any kind of information service, Judge Greene observed that those companies

> are currently permitted to compile and distribute "Yellow Pages" directories. If they were also allowed to provide their electronic counterpart, they would plainly have the incentive and ability to discriminate against the publishers of classified and other advertisements. . . . Since there would appear to be no economic basis for anti-competitive activity in connection with the production of "White Pages" directories, there is no reason under the decree why the [Bell companies] could not offer, in whole or in part, such directories in electronic form. Such an option will accordingly not be prohibited.[14]

This decision specifically rejected arguments by the Justice Department in favor of freeing the Bell companies' entry into information services.[15]

Under pressure from a higher court, Judge Greene was later forced to reverse his decision. The U.S. District Court of Appeals ruled that he could keep the Bell companies out of information services only if he could prove conclusively that anti-competitive behavior would result. Judge Greene responded that, lacking perfect foresight, he had little choice but to allow the Bell companies to enter the information services market. He did this with considerable reluctance, however, noting that in his view removing the information service ban on the Baby Bells was "incompatible with . . . the public interest."[16]

---

apparently a man of great integrity, and he is widely respected throughout the telecommunications community. He is also in an unenviable position, since he presumably never wanted to be a one-man regulatory board for the telecommunications industry. Nevertheless, this is what he has become.

[14]"Greene Finds Info Services Most Difficult," *Telecommunications Reports* 53, no. 37 (September 14, 1987): 37.

[15]Those arguments were brilliantly supported in a weighty report prepared by Peter Huber, but to no avail. See Peter W. Huber, *The Geodesic Network* (Washington: U.S. Government Printing Office, 1987). This book is interesting, informative, and amusing, adjectives that are seldom applied to a government report.

[16]"Greene's Info Services Decision Provides Blueprint for Appeals," *Telecommunications Reports* 57 no. 30 (July 29, 1991): 1. In fact, this decision simply shifted the debate over the role of the regional operating companies to Capitol Hill, where it is likely to remain for some time. The uncertainty arising from the battles being fought in the courts and in Congress will, in itself, act to restrain the Bell companies' ambitions and capabilities in the information-services market.

Surely there was something odd about keeping the Bell companies out of the electronic yellow pages business. Judge Greene and other proponents of such limitations have stated that their objective is to encourage the development of electronic directory services. But restricting the Bell companies in that area would ban from participation the very companies that have been most closely associated with providing directory information for decades.

On the other hand, the apparently innocuous decision to let the Bell companies supply electronic white pages has led to some surprising developments. In an era of convergence, definitions are no longer clear-cut. Electronic white pages are a lot more than just on-line versions of hard-copy white pages. Not so long ago, for example, US West caused some controversy when it proposed including ZIP codes and telephone area codes in its electronic white pages. The service offered by US West would also permit searches that retrieve a name and address associated with a telephone number or a name and telephone number associated with a particular address. Although US West's customers might appreciate such flexibility, its potential competitors in the on-line directory business did not. They said that the features offered by US West constituted manipulation of information content, which was specifically prohibited to the Bell companies in the MFJ.

US West defended its service by noting that Judge Greene had allowed US West and two other Bell companies to supply customer names and addresses if a caller to directory assistance provided a telephone number. US West argued that that was, in principle, the same service it wished to offer through its electronic white pages.

More is at stake, of course, than just on-line directory services. The ease with which digital information can be combined and manipulated will encourage the Bell companies to offer a broader range of services. If telephone companies offered on-line yellow pages, for example, it would be child's play to add to the listings for retail outlets information about the products carried there.[17] Interactive terminals could soon turn an information service into a

---

[17]Newspapers are one of the groups most adamantly opposed to telephone companies' offering any type of information or on-line directory services for precisely that reason. The ability to provide current information about products and prices through an on-line yellow pages service would undermine the demand for newspaper advertising that provides similar information.

home shopping service. Similarly, directory entries for movie theaters could easily include information about the films playing and the showtimes. Indeed, reviews of current movies could be added. Before long, telephone companies following this path would have a full-scale videotex service up and running.

Originally Judge Greene explicitly ruled out the possibility of the Bell companies' providing videotex service. He preferred that they be limited to providing what he called "introductory information" as part of a gateway to videotex service. In his model, such introductory services would have been strictly limited to displaying a welcoming page and a listing or directory of information providers.

The gateway concept is still alive and well in the video-dial-tone proposal. Identified with the FCC's former chairman Alfred Sikes, it is essentially a call to reaffirm the Bell companies' role as common carriers. Under this proposal, the telephone companies would be allowed to transmit video services, but others would provide the content. The video-dial-tone proposal is meant as a compromise. On the one hand, regulators hope to provide enough incentive to the large telephone companies to invest in fiber optics. On the other hand, they seek to protect broadcasters, cable-television operators, newspapers, and others who worry that they will lose business if telephone companies are allowed to assume the role of broadcasters.

Gateway services or video dial tones seem like a reasonable idea at first glance. But if we can no longer be sure quite what white pages are, how much more trouble will introductory information services represent? Traveling this road will almost certainly require that ever-finer distinctions be drawn by regulators as more and more detailed decisions are made about new services. This kind of regulatory nitpicking cannot help but be both controversial and arbitrary, and it will lead inevitably to reduced respect for the law and increased politicization of the regulatory process. Telecommunications regulation that dwells on such fine details cannot help but delay the introduction of new services. If anything undermines the public interest, surely that process does.[18]

Conclusion

In this chapter, we have begun to examine how convergence of the communications subindustries is affecting publishers and

[18]A key theme in this book is that telecommunications regulation delays and sometimes kills new and innovative services.

telephone companies, leading both to take on quasi-broadcasting characteristics. This convergence now threatens the central dogma of U.S. domestic telecommunications regulation—the three-segment model. Regulators everywhere are struggling to save that model and everywhere they are failing.

I believe there is a better way. I would suggest that the various players in the information services market should be allowed to compete, unfettered by government regulation and unaided by government support. In the next two chapters, I will show that the major objections to such a policy—the existence of local telephone monopolies and public ownership of the airwaves—are not well founded. We must also determine what kind of legal framework should be applied to the emerging information services. I believe new services should be governed primarily by the First Amendment. I shall return to that point in a later chapter.

3. The Myth of the Communications Monopoly

Politicians and bureaucrats love to meddle, and meddling with information technology is particularly attractive. Information is power, and power is sweet music to the collective souls of both groups. Politicians and bureaucrats still need to justify their control over information technology, however, and one of the most common excuses for intervention is the presence of monopoly power. Sadly, the general public still seems to believe that concentration of the resources within a particular industry is inevitably wicked and requires government intervention. A politician has to do little more than cry, "Monopoly!" and a million voices will respond, "Regulate it! Regulate it!"

The widespread fear of monopoly is also exploited by businessmen. Labeling a competitor a monopolist can be an effective, if cynical, piece of corporate strategy. Known monopolists are constrained through regulation in almost everything they do. It is frequently the case, of course, that conduct cited by a firm as evidence that its competitor is a monopoly is also a common business practice of the accuser.

It has long been argued that segments of the electronic communications business are natural monopolies. Throughout its history, regulation of the telephone industry has been predicated primarily on that claim. Contrary to what one might expect, as the traditional framework of telecommunications policy collapses under the weight of information technology convergence, claims of monopolistic practice are likely to increase and take on a new significance, helping to preserve the legitimacy of the regulators in an era when revolutionary technological change might otherwise make their efforts seem increasingly foolish. Accusations of monopoly will also be a competitive tool of increasing importance to firms in the information technology and service businesses as one way of keeping new competition at bay. Whining about monopoly can be an effective way of winning support from those who might otherwise be skeptical about the value of continued (or increased) regulation.[1]

The attitudes of owners and managers of electronic communications businesses are reminiscent of what the late Phil Ochs, the great protest singer of the 1960s, had to say about liberals. They are "ten degrees to the left of center in good times and ten degrees to the right of center when it affects them personally."[2] Communications industry magnates are great defenders of deregulation when it comes to what they can do individually. They are much less enthusiastic when deregulation means more competition for their companies.

The smaller long-distance telephone companies are a case in point. In many ways they have been the heroes of the telecommunications deregulation battles. Under the gutsy leadership of Bill McGowan, MCI led the good fight that broke the AT&T stranglehold on long-haul telephony in this country. But today, the smaller long-distance carriers are in the counterrevolutionary vanguard. Any suggestion that the FCC might loosen its grip on AT&T leads to forecasts of doom for telephone subscribers from the smaller long-distance companies.[3]

Nor are the long-distance telephone companies the only culprits. The cable-television companies, while fighting accusations that they themselves are monopolies, have staunchly opposed the local telephone companies' entering the cable business. In resisting telephone companies' encroachment into their markets, the cable companies have raised the specter of monopoly as a means of keeping the Bell companies out of the home video-entertainment-delivery business.[4]

[1]The trend toward an increased emphasis on regulation is already apparent. Congress recently reregulated the cable-television industry, bowing to arguments that cable television is a local monopoly, that it will supply low quality at high prices, and that only action by the federal government can save us from the evil cable-television operators.

[2]In his 1965 song, "Love Me, I'm a Liberal." Ochs, a Marxist, wrote many songs that would appeal to a libertarian.

[3]The old Bell companies are almost certainly further from winning an end to the restrictions on their entry into long-distance business than they are from gaining freedom from other line-of-business restrictions.

[4]The newspapers, fearing a loss of advertising revenues (especially classified advertising revenues), have also fought telephone-company information-service entry.

The regulatory strategy of the local telephone companies is somewhat different. The efforts of the regional Bell operating companies are geared more toward expanding the services they can offer than toward keeping others out of local telephony.[5] Not surprisingly, the local telephone companies are cautious about using the word "monopoly" in their regulatory campaigning. It would be all too easy for their opponents to brand them as pots calling kettles black. Still, the telephone companies will, from time to time, play on the public fear of monopoly by pointing out that their entry into new businesses would provide more competition or help break up existing monopolies.[6]

The political and legal battles between AT&T and other long-distance carriers or between the cable and telephone industries are evidence of how the very existence of telecommunications regulation skews the type of competition that takes place. Winners in the communications industry do not always conquer by designing an innovative new telecommunications service, by being more responsive to customer needs, or by offering lower prices. Winning often requires the loudest voice on Capitol Hill, at the FCC, or at the state public utilities commissions. That kind of victory may lead to significant benefits for communications companies and their shareholders, but it is far from clear that communications customers benefit at all.

In this chapter I will examine the question of communications monopolies. Communications monopolies do exist, and they are genuinely pernicious, but they are largely the creation of government and regulators and are not natural monopolies as commonly understood.

What Is a Communications Monopoly?

Like most political battle cries, accusations of monopoly make impressive rhetoric. A careful examination of the facts often raises doubts about the accuracy of the charge, however.

[5]Local telephone companies do occasionally gripe about the activities of alternative-access carriers, who provide point-to-point private-line connections in many downtown areas in direct competition with the telephone companies' own services. I will return to the growing competition facing telephone companies later in the chapter.

[6]These arguments make sense in the telephone companies' battles with the cable companies. Other lines of business the Bell companies would like to enter (such as information services, long-distance telephony, and equipment manufacturing, for example) are already relatively competitive.

Consider cable television, for example. The perception of cable television as a local monopoly is the putative basis for reregulating the industry. But if cable television is a monopoly, what exactly does the local cable operator monopolize? It is true that in many areas, certain programming is available only over cable. If you enjoy locally originated community programming, for example, you may have no option but to subscribe to cable. Furthermore, in most cities only one company offers cable service.[7]

That may not make cable television a monopoly, however. Many communities have only one source for a particular kind of product. Small towns often have only one book store, for example. Is that store a monopoly in need of regulation? Your answer will depend on your definition of monopoly, but a definition that includes any business in a given geographical area that is a single source of a particular product or service will uncover monopolies everywhere. Even if you could regulate all of them, many monopolies are hardly threats to the public interest, no matter how broadly defined.

The single local book store faces competition from alternative sources such as mail-order book clubs. Similarly, the local cable operator competes with other forms of television delivery systems. Most notably, cable competes with terrestrial (over-the-air) broadcasting by network affiliates and independent stations. Microwave-delivery and satellite-delivery systems are in some cases alternatives to cable television. Finally, you can always go to the video store and rent a movie.

Not all these options are available today in every location. Apartment and condominium dwellers are not able to install their own satellite dishes, although some building managers do install master antennas and distribute programming to tenants.[8] Still, virtually

---

[7]Of course, in virtually all of these cases, local governments prohibit more than one cable entrant. We will return to this later.

[8]Satellite television in the United States consists of (legally or illegally) receiving programming that is primarily distributed for the use of terrestrial broadcasters or cable-television operators. This programming is transmitted by relatively weak signals that need fairly large earth stations (satellite dishes) to receive them. In Europe and Japan, where cable television is not as widespread as in the United States, there are a number of direct satellite broadcasting systems that are specifically intended to broadcast to homes. They broadcast signals with sufficient power to allow them to be received by dishes a foot or so across. Such satellite dishes can be mounted in a window.

everyone has some choice among cable television, several terrestrially broadcast television channels, and videotape.

To many observers, the existence of those alternatives is simply not enough to refute the charge that cable companies are monopolies. That is so in part because many policymakers and regulators still compare real-world markets with the perfect-competition model when looking for market failures.

The perfect-competition model requires several players in a market offering virtually identical products. Consumers are assumed to be fully aware of everyone's products and prices, and in this model, it costs nothing to switch suppliers. The critical consequence of these assumptions is that no market rival can set his own price. Price is set by the marketplace. In a world of perfect competition, if any supplier attempts to charge a slightly higher price than his competitors, all of his customers will immediately desert him for the lower priced suppliers. Because all products are assumed to be identical, price is all that matters.

The perfect-competition model is largely a theoretical construct. No two businesses ever offer an absolutely identical range of services and products, and consumers never possess complete information about all the alternatives available. Further, even when comparing identical products—a particular make and model of car, for example—price may not be all that matters. Service, a dealer's selection of colors, or the manners of the salesman may influence a buyer's decision.

Regulators looking for markets that stray from the perfect-competition ideal will find them everywhere. Communications regulators searching for a monopoly to slay will find that many participants in communications markets can raise their prices without losing all their customers. Given that criterion, both cable television and the local telephone companies have long been targets of those who would control monopolies.

This approach to identifying monopolies is fairly plausible at first sight, but at its core, it is quite arbitrary. The key to identifying a monopoly by this method is in how a market or product or class of services is defined. Cable operators dominate only one particular class of video-entertainment programming. Local telephone companies do supply virtually all local switched-voice service,[9] but local

---

[9]At present the only widespread alternative to the local telephone company comes from nonwireline cellular telephone companies in areas that have two cellular com-

point-to-point connections are supplied by local telephone companies, long-distance companies, and so-called alternative access carriers.[10]

The convergence of the communications subindustries will tend to make the definitions on which monopoly status is based ever more arbitrary. But convergence is not really the worst of it. Regulators will continue to be able to draw some sort of seminatural boundaries between different kinds of telecommunications services for the foreseeable future. The real problem lies in defining what it means to be a dominant firm. It is virtually impossible to find a class of communications services that is supplied entirely by a single company, so it is necessary for pro-regulators to determine when a firm has such a large share of the business that it can be said to dominate a market.

What Makes a Firm Dominant?

The concept of a dominant firm has played a significant role in the recent history of telecommunications regulation. AT&T is subject to FCC oversight in the long-distance telephone-service business, for example, because AT&T is considered a dominant carrier with market power. As a dominant carrier, AT&T faces constraints nondominant carriers do not. Before offering new services or new prices on existing services, AT&T must file a tariff informing the FCC (and hence its competitors) of its plans, and AT&T must often await FCC approval before taking action. AT&T must also receive FCC authorization to construct, acquire, or operate new interstate facilities. Nondominant carriers are not subject to similar requirements.[11]

---

panies. (One cellular franchise is always awarded to the local phone company.) Few people would choose to use cellular telephone service exclusively, however. It is far more costly than conventional telephone service. Nevertheless, real alternatives to the telephone company are on their way to the market, as will be described later in this chapter.

[10]Under the terms of the Bell break-up the Baby Bells cannot offer long-distance services, but AT&T and the other long-distance carriers can be involved in local communications—and they frequently are. All the major long-distance companies provide local point-to-point links for their largest customers. Sprint is both a major long-distance provider and the owner of many local telcos. Although it would presumably produce immediate action by the Justice Department, there does not appear to be any reason why a long-distance carrier, even AT&T, could not acquire a regional Bell operating company.

[11]Many long-distance carriers do file tariffs with the FCC, even when not required to do so.

The Baby Bells also face special restrictions. Unfortunately, much of the regulation that governs the regional Bell operating companies seems designed to punish AT&T (with which they are no longer affiliated) for its pre-break-up wrongdoings. But some of the rules have punished all of us. Restrictions like those that curtail the Bells' ability to enter manufacturing have clearly had a negative impact on their ability to conduct proprietary research and development. That hardly seems good public policy at a time when major American high-tech companies are said to be losing their competitive edge.

All these restrictions raise questions about how we define dominance. The most obvious approach to finding a dominant firm is to look at the relative revenues of companies serving a particular market. Information about the revenues of large firms is readily available, and unlike some of the more esoteric mathematical functions used by economists to measure market dominance, sales revenues are widely understood—even by regulators, lawyers, and politicians.

Those who argue that AT&T is still a dominant carrier generally start by recounting the great disparity in the revenues between AT&T and its smaller competitors. In 1991, AT&T's long-distance revenues were $34.4 billion. Its closest rival, MCI, sold only $8.3 billion in long-distance services, U.S. Sprint achieved $5.4 billion in long-distance sales, and the fourth ranking long-distance carrier— Cable & Wireless—weighed in at under $0.4 billion.[12] There are another 300 or so long-distance carriers, most of which actually resell the services of the major long-distance companies. Taken together, they did not account for more than $7 billion in revenues in 1991.

Such evidence would seem to identify AT&T as the dominant long-distance carrier in any normal sense of the term. Measured by revenues, AT&T controls approximately two-thirds of the long-distance market. If that is not dominance, what is? Regulators and the antitrust community have traditionally been convinced by this kind of data.

---

[12]Ivan H. Shefrin and Daniel W. Edwards, *U.S. Industrial Outlook '93* (Washington: U.S. Government Printing Office, 1993), p. 28-7.

Despite the popularity of using relative revenues as a measure of market dominance and monopoly power, there are good reasons to question this approach. Its most important shortcoming is that it ignores the *potential* of smaller competitors.

Although potential competition cannot be assessed in an entirely quantitative way, quantitative measures can be brought to bear on the issue. John Haring and Kathy Levitz, two FCC economists, attempted to measure market dominance by comparing the total assets of the major long-distance carriers.[13] The picture that emerges when looking at companies' assets is very different from the picture painted by revenues. AT&T is still the leader, approximately 40 percent of the assets deployed in the long-distance industry being owned by AT&T, but the gap between it and the other two leading carriers is much closer than a look at revenues alone would indicate. MCI has 29 percent of the assets in the industry, and U.S. Sprint has 18 percent.[14] In fact, MCI's asset base is 71 percent of AT&T's, and U.S. Sprint's assets equal 44 percent of the leader's.

Of course, the attempt to measure market dominance by comparing competitors' assets still has flaws. Although the asset measure provides some information about potential, it says nothing about the manner and efficiency with which the assets are deployed.

In an ideal situation, we would analyze potential competition on a case-by-case basis, reviewing an individual company's assets against a broad range of quantitative and qualitative criteria. The biggest problem with such an approach, after working out how to accomplish it, is that regulators and the antitrust community look for objective, quantitative measures of dominance. Quantitative measures are more easily agreed on by disputing parties, and there are more than enough contentious issues in even the simplest antitrust case. But no careful analysis of the complex interplay of economics and technology that typifies today's electronic communications business can be based entirely on mere mathematics.

[13]John Haring and Kathy Levitz, "What Makes the Dominant Firm Dominant?" Washington, Federal Communications Commission, 1989. This paper is one of several Working Papers put out by the FCC's Office of Plans and Policy.

[14]These figures are based on 1988 data. Using 1988 data for revenues, AT&T accounted for about 75 percent of total long-distance sales, MCI produced 11 percent of 1988 long-distance revenues, and U.S. Sprint accounted for 7 percent of total sales.

Consider one example. It is generally acknowledged that in the future, networking technology will be based on the packet-switching techniques used in data networks rather than on the circuit-switching techniques used in today's telephone networks.[15] An attempt to assess the future potential of competitors in the long-distance communications market might consider, therefore, the potential of various competitors to deliver packet-switched services.

AT&T's efforts in the packet-switching market have not been very successful. Its first attempt to offer a range of advanced packet-switching services to corporate accounts fizzled, and the network it was building to support its effort is now history. AT&T has recently reentered the packet-switching service business with an advanced packet service called frame relay, but it was not the first to offer that service. Further, AT&T has bought all its packet-service switches from a little company named StrataCom, despite the fact that AT&T is one of the largest manufacturers of communications switches in the United States. Those do not sound like the actions of a dominant carrier.

Sprint, meanwhile, holds a strong position in the packet-switching business. A few years ago it bought Telenet, one of the two leading providers of packet-switching products and services. The company has since been renamed SprintNet, and it was one of the first carriers to offer frame relay. Furthermore, SprintNet is using switches it builds itself. Sprint may be third in the long-distance voice business, but it is way ahead as a packet switcher. Who can say whether AT&T will be the dominant carrier of the future?[16]

An even more complex picture of potential competition emerges when we look at the smaller long-distance carriers. SprintNet's closest rival in the packet-switching business is BT North America. This company does not currently offer conventional long-distance

[15]This is not the place to go into detail about the differences between packet switching and circuit switching, but roughly speaking, in circuit switching information is delivered in a continual stream over a physical circuit. In packet switching information is broken down into packets, and each packet is routed through the network to its destination, often over different paths. It is generally believed that to enable the networks of the future to handle voice, data, video, and still images, they will need to employ an advanced form of packet switching called "asynchronous transfer mode" (ATM).

[16]Sprint is also the world's largest provider of videoconferencing services through its Meeting Channel service. AT&T is a distant second.

services, but it is owned by British Telecom, one of the emerging titans in the global information-technology marketplace. Should British Telecom express an interest in entering the U.S. long-distance market, it could challenge AT&T's dominance. Another carrier of interest is WilTel. WilTel had just $376 million in revenues in 1990, but it pioneered the frame-relay business and the transmission of high-quality digital video for broadcasters.[17] Either of these activities could help win WilTel an important slice of the public carrier business over the next few decades.

Who's Afraid of a Communications Monopoly?

The preceding analyses may prove nothing, but they do show that AT&T is less dominant than its rivals and detractors sometimes suggest. Even the FCC has recognized AT&T's reduced market power, and during the early 1990s, the commission has eased AT&T's regulatory constraints accordingly. The more lenient attitude toward AT&T could easily be reversed by a future FCC, however. That raises the question of why it matters that a firm is dominant. What harm are dominant firms expected to inflict on society?

The most widespread concern is that firms that dominate a particular market can charge monopoly prices, that is, prices above those that would be charged in a more competitive market. Haring and Levitz summarized the commonly accepted belief: "The price under this type of industry organization [in which one firm dominates the market] is higher than would prevail under conditions of perfect competition. Thus the possibility exists that regulation might improve the efficiency with which resources are allocated."[18]

A growing number of economists have lost sympathy for that approach. Leading the attack on the traditional view of competition have been the "Austrian" economists,[19] who argue that the traditional economic models of perfect competition are too far removed

[17]The digital video transmissions were carried out through WilTel's subsidiary, Vyvx.

[18]Haring and Levitz.

[19]The Austrian school of economic thought derives its name from the fact that its founders were Austrians. Its principal modern proponents, Ludwig von Mises and Friedrich A. Hayek, were also Austrians. Both left Austria, however, and the Austrian school of thought is now as strong in the United States as it is in Europe, if not stronger.

from the real world to be of any practical use in defining what markets ought to look like. The only way to determine how a market should behave is to study a functioning market. Because there are no real-life perfectly competitive long-distance telephone markets, we cannot know whether or not AT&T or any other long-distance carrier is charging an excessive price.

This argument is often criticized as being naive. But it is important to understand what is not being said here. The Austrians and other economists critical of the perfect-competition model do not deny the existence of market power. Businessmen are certainly aware of the importance of clout in a market, and AT&T still has a lot of clout. It can get away with more than a smaller telephone company can, and pricing is just one aspect of its market power. AT&T can also negotiate better deals with suppliers and put more money into developing and testing new technologies.[20]

But although some firms are more powerful than others, and some firms are very powerful in specific markets, no private firm is all-powerful. If AT&T sets its prices too high, lets its quality fall too low, or offers products that do not meet the needs of end users, there will be other carriers who will recognize the opportunity and enter the market.[21] AT&T may be a dominant carrier today, but if it overprices its services or reduces its service level, it is unlikely to remain the dominant firm in the market for long.

The Communications Monopoly as a Government Franchise

Despite the promise of consumer protection inherent in market entry, we cannot dismiss the problems associated with communications monopolies. Many communications businesses are monopolies in the truest sense of the word—by grant of an exclusive government franchise.[22] Such monopolies are as a rule the most pernicious.

[20]According to some business strategists, gaining market power in this sense should be the central goal of businessmen.

[21]Network failures by AT&T during 1992 led some congressmen to urge the FCC to "do something." Suggestions included enhanced technical oversight of AT&T's network and fines for system failures. What the congressmen failed to realize is that the market had already done something: AT&T lost customers to other carriers because of its network problems. I would suspect that the threat of losing customers in large numbers is a much stronger incentive for AT&T to get its house in order than the threat of being fined or having bureaucrats tour its facilities from time to time.

[22]The meaning of the term "monopoly" that was first understood by English common law was a grant of special government privilege.

45

When a company is granted an exclusive franchise by the government, anti-consumer actions cannot invite market entry by definition. Poor service quality or higher prices by a government franchise may lead to investigations by the government, the press, or one or more consumer groups, but they do not substitute for market entry by a competing provider. Investigations help define the problem, but market entry solves it by supplying customers with an alternative.

There are several important examples of government franchise monopolies in the electronic communications business, although the most important example historically no longer exists. Before the 1982 settlement of the antitrust case against it, the unified Bell system possessed, for all intents and purposes, government-granted control of the lion's share of the U.S. telephone market. During the antitrust case that eventually broke up Ma Bell, one of the defense arguments was that she acted like a monopoly because the government had granted her monopoly status.

Even with the break-up of AT&T, exclusive government communications franchises abound. In local communications markets, franchises from state public utilities commissions or city governments remain a critical barrier to entry. That is true both for local telephone communications and for cable television. Even where the government allows entry by more than one supplier, competition is usually restricted to a narrow range of services.

Government franchising of local telecommunications monopolies is, of course, inevitably justified as being in the public interest. The most widespread argument is that local communications services represent natural monopolies. In other words, policymakers argue that if things were left to the market, one firm would dominate the market and charge monopolistic prices anyway. But if those markets are naturally monopolistic, it is not clear why state and local governments need to write laws or go to court to prevent new entry.

In reality, a political deal has been struck between the communications companies and their government overseers. The regulators offer the communications companies protection from competition. In addition, the traditional dependence on rate-of-return pricing regulation virtually eliminates the normal risks associated with new investments. State utilities commissions have typically guaranteed a specified profit regardless of how inefficient or ill-conceived investments were. Rate-of-return regulation seems to be on its way out, but price caps, the new and improved regulatory model, still seriously distort the signaling function of prices in the marketplace.

In return for protected markets and profits, communications franchisees provide a range of services specified by the franchiser— whether the federal, state, or local government. In the telephone industry the principle of universal service, a central plank of U.S. telecommunications policy, requires that telephone companies make basic voice service available to everyone in their service areas. Successful bidders for local cable franchises often must promise that they will supply locally originated or public-access programming as well as interactive services.

Defenders of the current system argue that everyone gains from such a quid pro quo. Local communications companies operate in an environment of reduced risk, and consumers get services that might not be available otherwise. It is not the free lunch it seems, however; there are important costs to be considered. First, it is not clear that franchise agreements provide consumers with choices they want. Second, the creation of government-protected local communications monopolies reduces consumers' alternatives. There is no place for consumers to go if they are dissatisfied with the service provided by a local telephone or cable company. Registering their disapproval may require giving up such services altogether. Finally, exclusive government franchises distort the competitive focus of affected companies to the general detriment of consumers.

Competition for Consumers or Competition for Favors?

The adage, "He who pays the piper calls the tune," accurately describes the situation facing many local communications companies. As long as government agents continue to award exclusive franchises in local communications markets, entry into the local communications business will mean winning the favor of government officials and regulators rather than impressing consumers. As a result, the uses to which communications businesses devote their resources will be shaped by the demands of government rather than by the demands of subscribers. Furthermore, because government-granted franchises generally mean that local communications businesses are protected from competition, entrants often have even less incentive to respond to consumers after they receive a franchise.

The local-origination and public-access services provided by cable television are good examples of the process of currying government favor. Government demands that successful cable franchises offer local-access channels may sound like nothing more than asking the cable television companies to be good local citizens. As Thomas Hazlett has pointed out, however, locally originated and public-access services have frequently been "extremely popular with citizens influential at City Hall, but virtually never watched by cable's ratepayers, and hence . . . highly unprofitable."[23] These politically preferred services have drained the financial and bandwidth resources of cable companies, reducing their ability to develop programs of more interest to their subscribers. Hazlett goes on to note that subsidized programming is only part of the effort to direct resources away from consumers and toward government decision-makers. Campaign contributions and free stock in local cable companies for politically powerful figures have been a frequent part of the competitive bidding process in the cable television industry.[24]

Monopolies, Convergence, Cable, and Telephone

Current U.S. telecommunications policy is extremely complex, in large part because rulemaking and legislation ultimately result in more rules, regulations, and legislation to offset the bad practices that stem from the first round of regulatory activity. The exclusive government franchise under which telephone companies operate—and the regulation of the subsequent telephone monopolies—is a good example of how messy things can get, especially in an era of convergence.

Having protected the markets and profits of local telephone companies, regulators must then protect the rest of the world from the monsters they have created. Specifically, regulators must prevent the telephone companies (telcos) from using their government-granted monopoly power to dominate other markets. That dominance might come through the telcos' use of their guaranteed profits

---

[23]Thomas W. Hazlett, "Should Telephone Companies Provide Cable TV?" *Regulation* 13, no. 1 (Winter 1990): 75.

[24]Ibid.

to subsidize ventures in other markets. Or it might come through the strategic use of local telephone networks to harm competitors.

It is not unusual, of course, for competing companies to have different costs of capital or different structural advantages. But the telcos' low cost of capital and their ability to use their networks to thwart competitors comes from regulation and not from the market as a reward for serving consumers particularly well. The Bell companies do have a government-created advantage, and those who would restrict the telcos' lines of business because of that advantage have a point.

But should we use further regulation to address a problem caused by regulation in the first place? A more straightforward, effective approach would be to simply deregulate local communications markets. The best way for the government to deal with a government-created monopoly is to stop empowering monopolists with exclusive communications franchises.

Regulators' response to such arguments is that the telephone companies cannot just be deregulated because they face no effective competition. That seems a strange argument coming from regulators who enforce the artificial barriers to new entry into the markets.

Despite continued government intervention, however, it is becoming more difficult to argue that there is no effective competition for local telephone companies. There are at least two important sources of potential competition in the local telephone markets. The first is the rapidly expanding alternative-access carriers. The second is local wireless communications.

Alternative-access carriers provide point-to-point communications in major downtown areas, linking buildings, providing local interconnections among long-distance companies' facilities, and connecting buildings with long-distance facilities. They emerged in the mid-1980s as a result of both deregulation and advancing fiber-optics technology, and they have grown rapidly since. According to the FCC, in 1987 alternative-access carriers accounted for just 133 route miles of fiber cabling. By 1991, they had 2,071 route miles in place.[25]

[25]Jonathan Krashaaur, "Fiber Deployment Update, End of Year 1991, Part II," *Fiber Optics Magazine* 14, no. 4 (April 1992): 25. "Route miles" refers to the amount of cable laid by alternative-access carriers. Analysts in the fiber-optic industry also use the term "fiber miles." A mile-long cable containing five fibers has a length of one route mile and five fiber miles. In 1987, the alternative-access carriers accounted for 7,700 fiber miles. By 1991, they accounted for 101,932 fiber miles.

A few companies are multiple-system operators. Teleport Communications, for example, is an alternative-access carrier with systems in Boston, Chicago, Los Angeles, San Francisco, Houston, and Dallas, as well as a regional network in the New York-New Jersey corridor. Metropolitan Fiber Systems (MFS) operates in Chicago, Minneapolis, Boston, Pittsburgh, Philadelphia, Baltimore, Houston, Los Angeles, San Francisco, New York, and Dallas. Several cities are home to more than one alternative-access carrier, so that in some areas large end users can buy their point-to-point communications from at least three suppliers.

Alternative-access carriers (also known as competitive-access providers) have generally been allowed to supply only point-to-point traffic. Switched services have been specifically closed to them. When alternative-access carriers were first getting started, such restrictions did not matter much. It was not clear that these companies would ever be in a financial position to construct multi-million-dollar switching centers. By 1991, however, the larger alternative-access carriers had indicated that they wanted to eventually offer most of the same services as the local telephone companies. Teleport has already installed its own switches in New York and Chicago, and the *Wall Street Journal* has quoted Teleport's director of regulatory affairs as saying, "Our ultimate goal is to become the second phone company in Chicago."[26]

To achieve their goals, the alternative-access carriers may need help from the regulators. Most important, they will need permission to enter the switched-service business. Potential competitors of the local telephone companies may also seek protection from the phone companies' efforts to keep them out of switched services by denying access to the local telephone networks.[27] Such potential abuses are often cited as a reason for continued regulation, at least in the short term.[28]

[26]John J. Keller, "Teleport Plans Tough Assault on Illinois Bell," *Wall Street Journal*, November 22, 1992, pp. B1, B3.

[27]Customers of Teleport would still want to be able to contact customers of Illinois Bell, for example, necessitating access to the phone company's network. Before the break-up of AT&T, but after the FCC had allowed MCI and others to enter the long-distance market, the local Bell companies were accused of providing inferior connections to customers using other long-distance companies.

[28]Of course, regulation designed to "level the playing field" is exactly the type of protection MCI and Sprint are so anxious to hold on to in their battles with AT&T

It should also be noted, however, that telephone companies and alternative-access providers are not in a perpetual state of war. In Chicago, for example, MFS and Teleport both resell Illinois Bell's Centrex service.[29] In other areas, competitive carriers often sell one another's services as backups for their own. That suggests that, with a little push from the regulators, the local telecommunications business could soon become very competitive indeed.

Furthermore, there are now services, such as frame relay, that use switches but behave like point-to-point private lines. Regulators who still prevent alternative-access carriers from offering switched services will soon be asked to determine whether they can offer frame-relay services. How public utilities commissions will view such questions is not at all clear.

The second source of competition in the local communications market is radio communications.[30] We are all familiar with cellular telephony as one kind of radio communications. In theory, a customer could subscribe to an independent cellular telephone service and avoid the local telephone company entirely; in that sense, cellular telephones represent competition for the local telephone company. The economics of cellular systems still tends to make them unattractive when compared to standard telephone service, however.[31]

Of much more importance is a spinoff from cellular known as personal communications services (PCS) or personal communications networks (PCNs).[32] PCNs are based on microcell technology,

---

in the long-distance market. I will discuss how this type of regulation should be phased out in the final chapter.

[29]Centrex service provides many of the features of a PBX (or private branch exchange). Customers who use Centrex service do not actually have to buy a PBX. The switching functions are carried out by the telephone company.

[30]I will discuss the regulation of radio communications more fully in the next chapter. Here I am concerned with radio communications as an alternative to the cabled communications provided by both the alternative-access carriers and the established telephone companies.

[31]The exception to this rule appears to be places where there is no existing cabled infrastructure. Local cellular systems can be installed more quickly than cabled systems, making them an attractive quick fix in many Eastern European countries attempting to modernize their communications systems.

[32]These terms are often used interchangeably, although strictly speaking, PCS is a set of services while PCN is the physical network providing them.

not radically different from traditional cellular technology. Microcells are spaced no more than 700 yards apart. The power levels they require for users to communicate with base stations is therefore much lower than what is required with conventional cellular systems. Lower power requirements, in turn, permit smaller, lighter phones that cost less than typical cellular phones. At this time, PCS remains unproven, but temporary licenses are being granted for trial services.

Some licenses have gone to alternative-access carriers, but the group most enthusiastically pursuing emerging PCS/PCN technology is the cable-television operators. In a classic example of convergence, cable operators see in the new technology an opportunity to make money at the expense of the telephone companies at a time when the telephone companies are threatening the cable-television franchise.

Regulators have so far responded inconsistently to these developments. Sometimes they have encouraged new technologies as a means of developing the communications infrastructure. Other times, in an apparent effort to protect the status quo, they have constrained communications companies' efforts to capitalize on new technologies. The result has been vague, indecisive, and arbitrary policymaking that has led to unceasing legal battles. Nowhere is this struggle more apparent than in the ongoing battle between the cable television and telephone industries.

The Cable-Telco Dispute

In 1970, the FCC adopted rules restricting telephone companies from providing cable-television service that said that a telephone company could not provide "video programming to the viewing public in its telephone service area, either directly, or indirectly through an affiliate owned by, or under common control with the telephone company." According to a paper published by the FCC:

> The Commission took this action in order to prevent local telephone companies from preempting the development of the cable television market and extending their local monopoly in local distribution through discrimination against non-affiliated cable television operators who needed access to telephone company poles and conduits.[33]

[33]Robert M. Pepper, "Through the Looking Glass: Integrated Broadband Networks, Regulatory Policies, and Institutional Change," Washington, Federal Communications Commission, 1988, p. 21. This is no. 24 in the Office of Plans and Policy Working Paper series.

In 1984, Congress codified these FCC rules in the Cable Communications Policy Act.[34]

The strictures against the telephone companies' entering the television business created little controversy at first. They fitted perfectly with the role that communications regulators had carved out for themselves as champions of the public interest against the monopoly power of the telephone companies. As convergence has destroyed traditional boundaries in today's technological environment, however, these rules have become the source of a deep-seated dispute between the cable-television and telephone industries. Their ongoing dispute has delayed the deployment of advanced technology in both industries, thereby preventing consumers and businesses from enjoying an expanded selection of communications services.

The technological origins of the dispute between cable and telcos lie in the use of fiber optics by the telephone companies. As I mentioned earlier, the cost of fiber-optic cable has fallen so that it now makes economic sense for telephone companies to use fiber in the local loop—the segment of their networks between the local telephone exchange and the subscriber's premises. In many cases fiber only runs part of the way to the home, but in others, the link between the exchange and the customer is now entirely fiber. Although it will be 50 years or more before copper telephone cables in the United States are completely replaced by fiber, both telephone companies and cable companies recognize that the use of fiber in the local loop will fundamentally alter the competitive environment in the local communications business.

The twisted-pair copper cabling that telephone companies have traditionally installed in homes and offices does not have the capacity to carry entertainment-quality video over extended distances. At best, twisted-pair cables can be used for a slow-scan video. The result is a rather ghostly image, adequate for a short videoconference but not for watching the movie of the week. Cable-television companies, on the other hand, use coaxial cable, which is more expensive than twisted-pair cable, but is capable of transmitting high-quality video signals.

---

[34]Among other things, this act banned cross-ownership of cable and telephone facilities within the United States. U.S. telephone companies can own cable systems in other countries, however, and some do.

Fiber cable is even better than coaxial cable as a video-transmission medium. The huge capacity of fiber-optic cables allows the highest quality digital video signals to be transmitted. As the telephone companies begin to deploy fiber in the local loop, they will also be creating the capacity to ship video into homes and businesses. Many experts believe that fiber will ultimately prove to be the optimal means of delivering high-definition television (HDTV).

In the early 1990s, fiber to the home is still relatively rare and largely experimental.[35] Many of the fiber telephone systems in place continue to provide only voice communications, and there are few signs at present that these experiments are about to evolve into major residential fiberization projects. Nevertheless, cable-company executives are worried.

If telephone companies are allowed to enter the video business, they will begin with a market penetration much higher than that of the cable companies. Almost everyone has a telephone, but only about 60 percent of television households have cable television. In addition, cable-company owners and managers are concerned about the economies that would accrue to telephone companies carrying both voice and video over their networks. A broader range of services would enable telephone companies to spread more widely the cost of building and maintaining their networks. Cable companies limited to video services must recover all their network costs from video customers. Telephone companies with fiber-optic systems might thus be able to eventually underprice traditional cable companies. Finally, cable-company executives are worried about competing with switched video services. To understand the implications of switched video services, it is necessary first to contrast the services currently offered by cable and telephone companies.

"Switching" refers to the process of connecting individual points in the network on demand. The telephone exchange (called a "switch" by those in the know) connects callers with those to whom they wish to speak. On a switched network, establishing connections between points on the network is a flexible process, and the connections can be held as briefly or as long as they are needed.

[35]Twisted-pair cables are very durable. Most telephone companies are in no hurry to replace cable that is still functioning adequately just to provide themselves with the capacity to supply services they are not yet allowed to offer.

In a cable-television system, there is a permanent connection between the cable operator's central broadcasting facility (the head-end) and every home the operator serves. All signals go to all homes all of the time. When you are watching channel 4 on cable television, channel 7 is coming into your home too. You do not see the program on channel 7 simply because you are not tuned to the necessary frequency. This is quite different from the situation on the telephone network. When you are speaking to your brother on the phone, you are not simultaneously receiving calls from your sister, your aunt, and a coworker.

The advantage of a switched service is that it allows for more efficient use of carrying capacity. Traditional cable companies use their transmission capacity to provide an array of channels to the homes they serve. For any individual home, however, capacity is being used to provide dozens of channels the inhabitants never watch. Switched video services would use the network's carrying capacity to a particular home or office to provide only what subscribers within that home or office wanted to see.[36]

Thus, the telephone companies' creation of a switched video system would allow for new services such as video-on-demand. This service would let you dial up any one of (literally) millions of movies, selecting your own starting times.[37] The same technology would also enable the development of switched-access television, with which viewers would be able to dial up one of thousands of special interest channels, allowing a level of "narrowcasting" that is impossible with conventional cable-television technology that broadcasts all channels to all subscribers.

In a recent book, George Gilder contrasted the potential of video narrowcasting and the limits of current broadcast television:

> The current system dictates that thousands of writers and directors labor to supply a few channels and distributors. . . . On the fringes of the television and film industries, however, American creativity is beginning to burst forth through VCRs, cable, low-power channels, public-television programs, low-budget movies and a huge variety of software. . . . These developments offer the merest

[36]Existing telephone company switches cannot provide television services, but television services can be added by interconnecting existing switches with specialized video switches.

[37]This service would also probably kill off today's video stores.

> glimpse of the possibilities. . . . Released from the restrictions of mass media, American culture could attain new levels in both the visual arts and literature.[38]

Gilder believes that narrowcast video would lead to increased numbers of intellectually stimulating or family-oriented programs. My own guess is that there would more likely be more avant-garde programs and pornography.[39] The technology would certainly allow for more of each, but as things stand now, we may never find out where increased control by consumers would take us.

Narrowcast video, video-on-demand, and other similar services clearly cannot be offered by telephone companies under the terms of the Cable Act as it now stands. The FCC has been attempting to find a way around this legal barrier, through its video dial-tone proposal for example, but it is not clear what the courts or even the FCC will finally allow when the inevitable legal battles begin.

Cable companies, meanwhile, face no legal or regulatory barriers to their offering video-on-demand or switched-access television services. But cable companies have no switches and only limited plans to install them. The biggest stumbling block is the multimillion-dollar cost of installing switching equipment. Generally speaking, cable companies lack any interest in developing the range of broadband services that would justify the introduction of switching equipment into their networks, although there are important exceptions to this rule.

Despite the profitability of new networking technologies, cable companies lack the financial capacity to try them out in multiyear trials and then abandon those technologies if they do not work out. The Bell companies, on the other hand, can conduct such experiments with virtually no impact on their bottom line. Although many accounts of the cable-telco dispute portray the two industries as equals, revenues for the entire cable-television industry in 1990 were only $17.8 billion.[40] The revenues for BellSouth alone were $14.4 billion in 1990.

[38]George Gilder, *Life after Television* (New York: Norton, 1992).

[39]In his book on the pioneering work being done at MIT on advanced television technology, Stewart Brand notes that the VCR's use for pornographic material was a major factor in its rapid adoption. See Stewart Brand, *The Media Lab* (New York: Viking Penguin, 1987), p. 28.

[40]Source: Paul Kagan Associates.

In fact, the cable-television industry is not a high-tech industry at heart. Its expertise lies in choosing and marketing programming. The physical networks used by cable television operators are effective, but in a sense they are also technologically crude. Some of the larger companies with multiple cable systems may have the resources to install some switches, and a couple are actually doing so. Other companies will use video-compression techniques to squeeze more channels onto their existing networks as a competitive response to video-on-demand and switched-access television services.[41]

In their growing competition with the telephone companies, cable television providers are not putting their greatest emphasis on technological responses, however. The cable industry's greatest effort is concentrated on lobbying Congress and the regulators to prevent the telephone companies from entering the video entertainment market. Of course, the telcos are lobbying just as hard for permission to expand into video services.

The lobbying efforts of both the cable and the telephone industries have been marked by more than a little hyperbole. Both sides have issued so-called technical papers promising to make the world a better place—or at least a more entertaining place—if only government decisionmakers see things their way.

The telephone companies have argued, for example, that in just a few years relative-cost considerations will justify installing fiber throughout their networks to provide voice services alone. The telephone companies hope to persuade state public utilities commissions and the FCC to support local fiberization on the grounds that it is part of the basic mission of the telephone companies, and thus an expense that should be paid for by all telephone subscribers.

---

[41]Extra channels provided through compression could allow for narrower broadcasting, but it is unclear how effectively compression will compete with switched video-on-demand. If compression is used to provide hundreds of channels, and if many of those channels are used for movies, then cable customers could potentially have hundreds of movie choices. With enough channels, popular movies could be shown simultaneously on several channels with different starting times, so that viewers would not have to wait long before their chosen movie began. The advantage of a switched video-on-demand service, however, is that the viewer does not have to wait at all. A movie selection is made, and the chosen movie begins when the viewer wants it to—just like renting a video.

Once in place, would we really want to let all that capacity go to waste?

It is true that the cost of fiber optics is falling while the cost of copper cabling is rising, and eventually it will make sense to replace all copper cables within the local telephone networks with fiber. But regulators have been right to question whether the cost differentials will justify replacing copper cabling over the next few years. In the age of convergence, there are fewer hard and fast rules about when technological improvements are cost-justified.

Cable companies have produced their own technical papers demonstrating that cable operators can provide fiber to the home for much less than the telephone companies can. The cable industry has argued that it will cost telephone companies a minimum of $1,500 to $4,500 per household to deploy fiber to the home. Cable operators, meanwhile, suggest that they can provide fiber services for $100 per house.

Such figures are misleading. The cost quoted by cable companies for their deployment of fiber represents just the cost of a fiber trunk cable amortized over the number of local cable-television subscribers. The figure used by the cable industry for the telephone companies represents the entire cost of a switched-fiber architecture. It is true that the cable-television companies do not need to bring fiber all the way to the home to deliver video services, but it is also true that if cable companies do not increase the technological sophistication of their networks by installing more than just a fiber trunk, they will be unable to deliver the kinds of advanced services planned by the telephone companies.

The propaganda war between cable and telcos is an example of how regulation turns what should be commercial competition into a political battle. In fact, without all the government restrictions and rulings, I believe that the whole wasteful and intellectually bankrupt dispute between the cable and telephone industries would never have occurred.

There is a natural community of interest between the cable-television and telephone companies. The telephone companies are more sophisticated than the cable companies when it comes to networking, but they have no experience in programming.[42] On the other

---

[42]Of course, there should be no legal restrictions preventing telephone companies from packaging programming should they wish to do so.

hand, program packaging is the area where the cable companies excel. Without government interference, an eclectic industry structure for local video distribution might well grow up, designed to fit the needs of local markets. In some areas, telephone companies would supply both the video programming and the channels through which that programming is carried. In others, cable companies would supply programming through the telephone-company networks. In some instances, cable companies would be affiliates or even subsidiaries of the telephone companies while in other cases, they would be customers. In a few areas we might see cable companies upgrade their own networks with switching gear to enable them to offer the kinds of advanced voice and video services that seem today to be the sole province of telephone companies.

Some cooperation between telephone companies and cable-television companies can be found even today. Smaller independent cable operators have been willing to cooperate with the telcos in their fiber-to-the-home experiments. Some of the larger multiple-system operators, who see their role primarily as video-entertainment service providers, admit privately that they do not feel especially threatened by the telephone companies. Many cable-television companies that are family businesses have reached a stage where their owners would like to sell all or part of their stock, and they would welcome the entry of the telephone companies into cable television because it would increase the demand for their stock.[43]

Although it is true that most cable-television interests today see the telephone industry as the enemy, in an economically freer environment cooperation between cable and telephone might flourish. And where there was not cooperation, there would be competition for consumer dollars rather than for government favors. The impact of regulation in this area is evident in the empty rhetoric, in the resources allocated to political lobbying rather than to meeting consumer demand, and in the delays in providing what are now technologically feasible new services. In fact as the FCC has loosened up some of its rules governing telco activity in video,

---

[43]Some cynics believe that what this group of cable operators would really like to see are rules that prohibit telephone companies from establishing their own cable systems but allow them to buy existing cable operations.

we have seen such cooperation, notably US West's investment in Time Warner.

The Regulatory Response

The FCC's friendliness to the telcos' plans for video is evidenced by its sponsorship of the video dial tone. The commission is also increasingly comfortable with the idea of common ownership of cable systems and telephone companies. The FCC has treated such arrangements with sympathy for some time.

Several years ago, over the strong objections of the cable-television industry, the FCC allowed a GTE subsidiary to supply cable-television service to a GTE fiber-to-the-home trial. More recently, over the objections of the telephone industry, the FCC allowed Cox Communications, a multiple-cable-system operator, and Teleport Communications, an alternative-access carrier, to jointly own several cable-television systems in areas where Teleport operates. The FCC cannot simply abandon the Cable Act's restrictions on cross-ownership, but it has interpreted the act as liberally as possible. It has also publicly acknowledged that it favors repeal of the statutory cross-ownership restrictions.

Ultimately, we must look to Congress to allow more freedom for telephone companies seeking to distribute video services. Legislative proposals that would give telephone companies a freer hand in that area are welcome news, but we should not expect too much.

In the first place, some legislators may feel they benefit from the continuing debate. As Thomas Hazlett has pointed out:

> It is clearly in the interests of some decisionmakers to delay a resolution. Congressional hearings are an excellent platform from which to gain publicity and influence, and the political consequences of action cannot be measured too hastily. A hurried policy decision would likely prove a suboptimal political decision.[44]

In the second place, part of the congressional momentum for telephone deregulation over recent years came from a perception that the cable industry was charging too much and making too much money. Advocates of increased freedom for telephone companies attempted to sell their program as a means of increasing

[44]Hazlett, p. 80.

the competition faced by cable operators and keeping their rate increases in check. In late 1992, Congress chose instead to reregulate the cable-television industry.

Cable television is not an unprofitable business, but cable-television companies are often highly leveraged, and the market for basic cable services is relatively mature. Reregulation could prove a serious blow to many cable companies, and some owners may seek buyers for their properties.

Deregulation of the telephone industry, if it occurs, coupled with reregulation of the cable industry, could speed acquisition of cable companies by telephone companies, and that in turn would allow the telephone companies to deploy their video services at a faster rate. But those trends, if left unchecked, could leave the telephone companies as the dominant players in local video-entertainment markets. If entry into the market is relatively free, their dominance will create no particular economic problems. Its political acceptability is another matter, however.

A single telephone company offering voice and video services is a long way from the model most legislators envision. Policymakers would prefer a world in which cable companies and telephone companies compete for the same subscribers. In the absence of such competition, legislators could become convinced that the telephone companies are monopolizing the local video-distribution market. Future debates could well center on the need to reregulate the telephone industry, starting the same vicious cycles again.

Conclusion

It is widely accepted that monopolies permeate the communications industry. But the traditional definitions of a monopoly either as a firm that controls all or virtually all of industry revenues or resources, or as a firm able to charge prices above normal have proved generally unsatisfactory and frequently incoherent, forcing us to fall back on the older definition of a monopoly as an exclusive government franchise.

Using that definition, there are a lot of communications monopolies around. It is unfortunate that so few government officials see the irony inherent in regulating in the public interest the monsters they have created by granting government-protected franchises, which are not in consumers' interest. The existence of communications monopolies slows the introduction of new and innovative services by the industry. The cable-telco dispute is just one example of how government-created monopolies and misguided antitrust action can delay new services. It is also a good example of how deregulation in name only will fail to deliver the advantages brought by truly free markets. As long as cable companies or telephone companies enjoy government-protected franchises, they will remain oriented toward political rather than economic ends.

In chapter 6 I will argue that electronic communications should be demonopolized. The telephone and cable companies should be allowed to act like any other business, unfettered by the regulatory ties that now bind them. Before discussing the implications of that proposal, however, I will examine another of the untouchables of U.S. telecommunications policy—the belief that the airwaves are public property held in public trusteeship, to be allocated by the government.

4. Who Should Own the Airwaves?

One of the most widely accepted doctrines of U.S. telecommunications policy is that the government should have an ongoing role in managing those segments of the electromagnetic spectrum that are used for radio communications.[1] Rather than creating true property rights in the spectrum, however, the government first allocates spectrum to particular applications (e.g., to broadcast television, land mobile radio, or direct broadcast satellite) and then assigns parts of the spectrum to individuals or organizations that wish to use the spectrum for the specified purpose. Spectrum allocations and assignments are temporary. The government retains the right to reallocate both spectrum and licenses as technical or political considerations demand. Radio and television stations receive broadcast licenses for a limited number of years, for example, and there are constant requests for the FCC to reallocate spectrum to new or expanded uses.

Most people in the telecommunications community and outside it seem to believe that this state of affairs is reasonable, and government management of the spectrum certainly has a long history. But despite its age and wide acceptance, the doctrine that the airwaves are a public good best dealt with by the government acting as a public trustee is in error, and it has unfortunate consequences.

As with the acceptance of communications firms as natural monopolies, the belief that the airwaves are essentially a public good has always been mistaken. In both cases, new technology has made what was once merely misguided policy increasingly untenable. There are three major problems with the current system. First, spectrum is not a natural resource in the usual sense, nor is it a scarce resource in the sense that using it uses it up. Second,

---

[1]The term "radio" is used here in the technical sense to include all communications propagated over the air through electromagnetic radiation, including terrestrial microwave and satellite communications as well as the UHF and VHF bands associated with television broadcasting stations.

centralized spectrum management slows technological development and politicizes spectrum management. Finally, old bad arguments for government control of the spectrum are being replaced by new bad arguments for government control.

The Radio Communications Environment

Although more and more electronic communications travel over wire, cable, and fiber, much of it still travels over the airwaves. Despite the growing presence of cable television, for example, approximately 40 percent of American viewers still pick up television programming on a UHF or VHF antenna. Even cable television systems use some over-the-air transmission. Much of the programming distributed over cable is delivered to the cable headend by satellite or (occasionally) by microwave transmission.[2] Satellite and microwave transmissions also play an important role in the long-distance telephone system, especially in international communications where satellites are still vital, and radio communications are likely to become increasingly important as a source of growing competition in the market for local telephone services.

Similarly, the airwaves are the only communications medium available for mobile communications. What is more, mobile communications are playing a growing role in the total communications environment, the clearest example of the trend being cellular phones. Ten years ago, few civilian vehicles had radiotelephones; now there are millions of cars equipped with them. Advancing satellite technology is also bringing us phones on aircraft and trains. For the ultimate in mobile communications, experts predict that eventually there will be Dick Tracy–like wristwatch phones, capable of communicating with anyone, anywhere.

In short, policies toward radio communications and spectrum use are taking on increasing importance with advancing technology, and the politically based spectrum allocation system is having difficulty keeping up. The FCC's decision to allow companies and individuals to use particular chunks of spectrum for new and innovative services precisely because they are new and innovative is symptomatic. The method of parceling out spectrum known as

---

[2]As noted in chapter 3, the headend is the central point of the cable system from which signals are sent to subscribers.

"Pioneers' Preference" is helpful, but the ongoing management of spectrum by government is much more contentious.

How the Spectrum is Governed

Spectrum management in the United States is shared between the FCC and the National Telecommunications and Information Administration (NTIA), a part of the Department of Commerce that manages the use of spectrum by the federal government.[3]

Within the FCC, spectrum management is further divided according to application. The FCC's Mass Media Bureau manages the licensing process for the broadcasting spectrum, its Common Carrier Bureau distributes cellular radio-telephone licenses, and the Private Radio Bureau manages the licensing process for the nonsatellite land mobile services provided by companies other than common carriers. Each bureau has its own way of allocating and assigning spectrum. For example, assignments for cellular services are made by lottery, while assignments for broadcasting stations are made according to the technical, financial, and even ethnic characteristics of potential licensees.

The telecommunications industry has become increasingly aware of the inefficiencies that bedevil the traditional methods for allocating and assigning spectrum. Accordingly, there is a search on for improved techniques. There have even been some limited attempts to get the government out of the business of spectrum management.

FCC rules permit private groups using certified coordinators to manage some spectrum assignments in the private land mobile radio service.[4] Private groups have also played a role in coordinating the sharing of spectrum by satellites and terrestrial microwave systems. There has even been some privatization of the allocation process through FCC decisions allowing providers of certain mobile radio services to buy channel capacity from licensees in other service categories. Privatization of the airwaves still has a long way to go, however.

---

[3]This division of authority was laid down, like most of the basic rules governing telecommunications, in the Communications Act of 1934. I will focus primarily on the FCC's activities.

[4]This practice was explicitly recognized by Congress in the 1982 amendments to the Communications Act.

Justifying Government Spectrum Management

The government's ongoing role in spectrum allocation and assignment is based primarily on the notion of spectrum scarcity. Justice Felix Frankfurter reflected the accepted wisdom when he remarked, "Radio facilities are limited; they are not available to all who may wish to use them; the radio spectrum is not large enough to accommodate everybody."[5] Although Justice Frankfurter was talking about radio stations, it is generally accepted that much the same can be said about television stations, radio telephones, satellite communications, or terrestrial microwave transmission in telephone networks.

Economists argue that virtually all goods are "scarce," but in the United States we do not see government allocation of steel or bread. Indeed, markets exist to allocate scarce goods and resources.

The airwaves are viewed differently because they are considered a natural resource. Even in a capitalist economy, the government is generally viewed as having a role in protecting natural resources such as parks, rivers, and mountains. As just one more natural resource, it is argued, the government also has a role in overseeing the use of the spectrum.

Looked at in this way, spectrum management often becomes a sort of environmental issue. Supporters of the need for government supervision of the spectrum take the position that the electromagnetic spectrum is a gift of God or of Nature, and as such should not belong to anyone. Before deregulation and privatization took hold at the FCC in the 1980s, for example, the commission's chief scientist and head of its Office of Plans and Policy testified that the spectrum was "part of a subset of natural resources that do not conform to legal or geographic boundaries." The argument has also been made in more poetic terms. Some years ago, a popular book on electronic communications appeared with the title *Who Owns the Rainbow?*[6]

One does not need a doctorate in physics to understand that there are obvious differences between rainbows and radio communications, although both are manifestations of the electromagnetic

[5]Quoted in Ayn Rand,"The Property Status of Airwaves," in *Capitalism: The Unknown Ideal* (New York: Signet, 1967), pp. 122–23.

[6]Hal Glatzer, *Who Owns the Rainbow?* (Indianapolis, Ind.: Howard W. Sams, 1984).

spectrum. But such metaphors demonstrate how easily policy debates regarding spectrum allocation can become muddied and confused.

Even Herbert Hoover, generally not thought of as one who held socialist views, accepted government oversight of the spectrum as natural. Ayn Rand, in her article, "The Property Status of Airwaves," quotes him as having said:

> Radio communication is not to be considered as merely a business carried on for private gain, for private advertisement, or for entertainment of the curious. It is a public concern impressed with the public trust and to be considered primarily from the standpoint of public interest in the same extent and upon the basis of the same general principles as other public utilities.[7]

Hoover was, in fact, influential in establishing the Federal Radio Commission from which the whole body of spectrum regulation ultimately grew.

Are the Airwaves Really Scarce?

As it turns out, the claim that radio communications are akin to a natural resource is incorrect. In the first place, the term "airwaves" is a misnomer. Air is not involved. Radio communications use not air, but electromagnetic radiation—oscillating electric and magnetic fields that move through space at the speed of light. This phenomenon is natural in the sense that it is a manifestation of the laws that govern nature, and sometimes such radiation occurs naturally. Rainbows, thunder, solar activity, and static electricity on your clothes or carpet all involve natural discharges of electromagnetic radiation that occur costlessly, without involving any deliberate human action.

It is with respect to human action that radio communication is nothing like rainbows, thunder, solar activity, or static electricity. Radio communications use electromagnetic radiation deliberately created for the purpose, often at a high cost. A satellite communications system may cost hundreds of millions of dollars, for example. By contrast, the benefits of the rainbow are available to all of us without any human intervention or expense whatsoever.

[7]Rand, p. 125.

67

Advocates of spectrum management as ecology recognize all this, of course, but they do not consider the differences in the processes by which we obtain the benefits of rainbows and radio communications to have any bearing on the ownership of particular chunks of bandwidth. Proponents of public management of the spectrum simply assert that the sources of both should be publicly owned. Nothing is really changed by asserting the public's ownership of a rainbow, but in the case of radio communications, public ownership requires a public trustee to allocate and assign bandwidth. Hence, government becomes a major player in the radio communications market.

The second myth has to do with the scarcity of spectrum. Electromagnetic radiation is not a resource in radio communications in the normal sense of the term. Radio communications use electromagnetic radiation, but they do not use it up. In fact, all transmitters used in radio communications systems are designed specifically to create electromagnetic radiation.

Although there is no scarcity of electromagnetic radiation for use in radio communications, there is competition for the right to carry out radio communications at certain frequencies and powers and in certain geographical areas. Anything for which there is competition can be said to be scarce in some sense, and it is in this sense that the spectrum used for radio communications is scarce.

Scarcity and Interference

Spectrum scarcity has a rather precise meaning. If two individuals or groups of individuals within a certain area try to send communications signals at the same frequency, they will interfere with each other, making communications by either party impossible. In most areas there are a lot of potential users of technically attractive frequencies. It is in this sense that the airwaves (or more precisely the spectrum of electromagnetic radiation) is a scarce resource. Proponents of government control argue that the private sector could not successfully allocate spectrum in a way that avoids interference.

The size of the area over which interference will make itself felt depends on the power of the transmission. The low-power base station for a cordless phone does not (in theory) generate enough power to interfere with a similar base station in the house next door, for example. On the other hand, two television stations in the same town would normally have enough power to jam each other if they were to broadcast on the same frequency.

Regarding spectrum scarcity in this way has some important implications. For one thing, spectrum scarcity can be obviated by technological means. If a transmitter can be used with less power in a particular communications application, spectrum becomes less scarce in the sense that the frequencies used by one application can now also be used by another at a closer geographic distance. If an application can be made to work over a narrower bandwidth, frequencies are opened up for other uses. More frequency also becomes available when new technology allows use of frequencies higher than those previously employed in radio communications.

These trends have been apparent throughout the history of radio communications, but they have accelerated in the past few decades. Low-power television stations serving small communities or neighborhoods, indoor radio data-communications networks for offices, and cellular-telephone networks are all outgrowths of the development of low-power transmission technology. Even more important, new technology is allowing applications to be crowded into ever smaller bandwidths.

Consider recent developments in digital communications. A 64 kilobit per second (kbps) channel—a digital communications channel through which 64,000 bits of information travel every second—is the official international standard for one two-way voice conversation. When that standard was introduced, 64 kbps really did represent the amount of bandwidth needed for high-quality voice communications, but technology has improved since then. Voice communications can now be compressed sufficiently so that four or even five voice channels can be squeezed into a single 64 kbps channel. New techniques for compressing video images have also been developed so that entire videoconferences can be conducted over 64 kbps channels. Video is a notorious user of bandwidth, and just a few short years ago the result of compressing a video signal down to 64 kbps would have been a barely perceptible image on the screen. With today's technology, the quality of the image is not exactly high-definition television, but it is adequate for short videoconferences.[8]

[8]The videoconferencing discussed here is so-called slow-scan videoconferencing that uses desktop equipment. Near-broadcast quality video is also available, but it uses much higher bandwidths.

Finally, new technology is also pushing up the frequency range within which practical radio communications are possible. Before World War II, radio communications were mostly found in the lower reaches of the spectrum, where radio and television broadcasts still take place. The development of radar, however, led to new technology allowing radio communications at higher frequencies—frequencies in the so-called microwave range. The advent of microwave communications technology changed the economics of long-distance telephony, ultimately undermining AT&T's long-distance monopoly. It also led to the development of satellite communications. Satellites are little more than big microwave relays in the sky, and experimental satellites are today testing communications at even higher frequencies, in the upper reaches of the microwave and beyond.

With lower-power communications, data compression, and practical communications at high frequencies, spectrum may still be scarce, but it is not as scarce as it once was, and it is becoming less scarce all the time.

Radio Communications as a Unique Medium

Proponents of government spectrum management have other arguments in their arsenal, however. Radio communications are also presumed to be unique in the sense of having no close substitutes that perform similar functions. If the tasks we accomplish with radio communications could easily be accomplished by other means, spectrum scarcity would not be an issue.

At least in the case of fixed (nonmobile) communications, there is reason to question the uniqueness of radio communications. There seem to be plenty of close substitutes. To their dismay, terrestrial (over-the-air) broadcasters have found out just how close a substitute transmissions over coaxial cable can be, as cable-television companies have eaten into their market share. The transmission medium for long-distance telephone communications is equally open to substitution. Originally, long-distance calls, like all telephone communications, were carried over copper cables. During the 1960s and 1970s, the transmission media of choice for the long-distance companies shifted to radio communications using satellites and terrestrial microwave. Now long-distance companies are turning to fiber-optic cable.

Radio communications have a more secure place when it comes to mobile communications. Clearly, we cannot attach cables to the ends of trucks, cars, trains, boats, or planes to provide communications links. Still there may be some competition between radio communications and other links. The most obvious example would be consumers' choices between installing a cellular car phone and relying on pay phones. For many users, the latter option is still quite acceptable.

In short, where reasonable substitutes exist for radio communications, spectrum scarcity is not a problem. If radio communications are unavailable or highly priced, alternatives can be used. The more alternatives there are, the less scarce spectrum really is.

The most common substitute for radio communications is obviously cabled communications, and here there is no scarcity of bandwidth. Few geographic areas could support as many as 40 terrestrially broadcast stations without interference, but modern cable-television systems regularly offer twice that number of channels. Fiber-optic cables represent even more dramatic potential. Highly sensitive fiber-optic systems, called coherent systems, will be in commercial use in the next few years and will be capable of delivering to a single location 10 times the amount of bandwidth now allocated by the FCC for *all* radio communications applications.

With such developments in fiber optics, we appear to be moving into an era of spectrum abundance. But such abundance does not really depend on high-tech innovation; it is the nature of cabled (as opposed to radio) communications. When compared with the interference associated with radio communications, the interference problems generated by electromagnetic radiation encased in a cable are insignificant. Lack of spectrum thus becomes a nonproblem. If you need more capacity badly enough, simply lay another cable.

In short, there are no technical reasons for continued regulation of the communications market. Scarcity may be less of a resource problem in communications markets than in other industries, and the number of substitutes for radio communications is multiplying rapidly. It is not simply that there are no benefits to government spectrum-management, but that there are real and growing costs to government involvement as well. In particular, government oversight has significantly slowed technological progress.

The Government as Spectrum Manager: Sloth and Politicization

The present government role in allocating and assigning spectrum for communications not only represents the consensus view of how things should be done, but is also the law. The 1934 Communications Act specifically requires that the FCC take public-interest considerations into account in managing the spectrum. One could argue that the best way for the FCC to serve the public interest would be to turn the whole matter over to the marketplace, but that is clearly not what the framers of the Communications Act had in mind. And while government involvement in spectrum management has always slowed the development of new telecommunications services and politicized the process of spectrum assignment, those problems have become increasingly burdensome as technology has advanced more rapidly.

Slowing the Development of Services

The FCC is not an agency noted for the speed with which it makes decisions, and the more disagreement there is, the longer the FCC takes to reach a resolution. Unfortunately, disunity in the electronic communications industry is increasingly the norm.

Delays in the FCC's decision-making process are not surprising. Although it is reasonably well run and staffed with exceptionally intelligent men and women, its proceedings are governed by the Administrative Procedures Act, which requires that the commission hear from all interested parties and apply the public-interest standard in allocating and assigning spectrum. Assignment is usually a shorter process than allocation, but both processes can take years.

Consider the case of cellular telephones. The first proceeding to allocate spectrum for cellular telephony began in 1968. Seven years later—in 1975—the spectrum allocation was made. Six years after that—in 1981—the first commercial cellular license was granted. Nor did the process become automatic once the first license was assigned. In granting cellular licenses in the nation's 30 largest communications markets, the comparative analysis of nonwireline cellular applications (i.e., applications submitted by firms other than telephone companies) took on average 412 days (or 13.7 months) from a hearing date's being set to the granting of a construction permit.

The slow introduction of cellular services was clearly not a result of technical or market-related issues. The basic technique for cellular communications was actually invented in the late 1940s, although it was not until the 1960s that computer technology had advanced to the point where it could be practically implemented. By the 1960s, there was little doubt of the demand for cellular service. People were on waiting lists for years to get radiotelephones.

Clearly, it was the FCC process that delayed carphones for 13 years, and the cellular story is not unique. The new low-power personal mobile communications technologies discussed in chapter 3 were delayed by the FCC because parceling out spectrum for new services is always limited by old FCC decisions. If a chunk of spectrum technically suited for a new service has already been allocated for some other use, the FCC faces a choice. It must either disenfranchise the existing users of the old service, or it must find another chunk of spectrum for the new service.

When resource-allocation decisions are made by governments rather than by markets there are always lengthy delays. First, spectrum users threatened with disenfranchisement will fight reallocation tooth and nail. Second, allocation of spectrum outside of the market process is inherently arbitrary in the sense that technical information is seldom sufficient to provide a definitive solution to a spectrum-allocation problem. At best it suggests a number of alternative solutions, among which the authorities must then choose. In such situations, delays are inevitable as lengthy hearings are held so that all interested parties will have an opportunity to present their points of view. When decisions are finally made, there is always a question about whether the outcome is truly in the public interest and not just the result of the winners' hiring the more talented advocate.

By contrast, if spectrum allocation were left to market forces, the providers of new services would bid directly for the spectrum owned by existing users. Whether the existing user decided to hold on to his spectrum or sell it would depend on whether the new or the existing user valued the spectrum more highly, which in turn would presumably depend on which use had more profit potential.

A market system does not guarantee new users access to what engineers might consider the optimal part of the spectrum. Indeed, markets do not guarantee new users access to any part of the spectrum. But the bid-and-offer process is unlikely to take more than a couple of months, and it might take just a day or two. Nor is it final. As market and technical conditions change, so will the values attached to different parts of the spectrum by users. No conceivable FCC-based spectrum-allocation method could ever be as speedy or as flexible.

The Politicization of the Spectrum

Market-based decisions would also take the politics out of spectrum allocation and assignment. Politicization not only slows the deployment of new services, it also adds political connections as a decision variable to the technical and economic considerations. Although politics affect both spectrum allocation and assignments, the influence of political power is much more apparent in assignments of spectrum to particular users than it is in the allocation of spectrum to particular applications or services.

William B. Ray's book *FCC* provides an insider's account of how decisions are made at the commission.[9] Ray chronicles in depth the financial corruption that has marked the FCC since its founding as well as the twists and turns of FCC policy on what constitute good taste and the proper use of the airwaves.

Ray's chapter on political influence begins with a story from 1936 about Franklin Roosevelt's intervention in helping a friend of his obtain a radio-station license. All the president had to do, it seems, was to make a call to the chairman of the FCC. Intervention in the assignment process has not been limited to any single political party. During the Eisenhower administration,

> eight outspokenly Republican newspapers . . . received TV licenses and ten Democratic newspapers were denied them. . . . No Republican papers lost comparative hearings except where they were opposed by more powerful Republican interests. Conversely, no important paper that supported Adlai Stevenson for president won a comparative TV case.[10]

Ray also relates the story of how Lyndon Johnson built his broadcasting empire with a few assists from his friends at the FCC.

Ray's book covers only broadcasting policy, and most of the stories of political cronyism are from some time ago. But surely

---

[9]W. B. Ray, *FCC* (Ames: Iowa State University Press, 1990). This is also one of the few books on communications regulation that I would recommend to a layman.

[10]Ibid., p. 45.

few people would be surprised to find that political connections still count in the allocation and assignment of spectrum for both broadcasting and nonbroadcasting purposes. Because everyone agrees in principle that political influence coincides with the public interest only by coincidence, everyone should also agree that the kinds of abuses about which Ray writes are intolerable. There is no agreement, however, about what should be done. Ray appears to believe that the problem would be solved if only the FCC took its role as a public trustee a little more seriously.

This is surely naive. The persistent role of political favoritism in spectrum management through periods covering administrations of different political complexions suggests that this is a problem of institutions, not individuals. If a handful of politically appointed commissioners is given the task of allocating and assigning valuable bandwidth on the basis of the public interest, it is inevitable that political influence will become a significant factor in how those allocations and assignments are made.

The problems with politicization of spectrum management do not end with deciding who uses the spectrum to provide what communications services. The task of assigning and allocating spectrum in the public interest gives government decisionmakers both an excuse and a mechanism for controlling the content of the information carried on the airwaves. In fact, the Communications Act empowers the FCC to consider the character of prospective station owners before assigning broadcast licenses.

The idea of political appointees' passing judgment on the content of transmissions and the moral worth of those who do the transmitting is not a very attractive one. But a few of the right anecdotes can make it sound benign and perhaps even helpful. Ray's book is full of such anecdotes. He tells, for example, of how "our government ultimately was able to silence . . . [the] medical quacks" that beset early radio.[11]

Presumably the point of giving the government the right to silence medical quacks is to avoid the potential harm that could come from following such quackery, and faced with a choice between medical quacks and government regulation, some quite reasonable people might choose regulation. But the FCC's powers

[11]Ibid., p. 125.

extend far beyond instances in which some direct physical harm is likely to result. The broad nature of the FCC's role in content regulation is exemplified by the commission's long and active interest in the sexual content and general offensiveness of broadcast material.

It is widely accepted that the FCC's actions in cases of obscenity and indecency are similar to its actions in cases of medical quacks. Although civil libertarians may find the very power of the FCC itself objectionable, the end result does not smack of horrifying censorship. Consider, for example, the 1973 Pacifica case. The FCC objected to the Pacifica radio station WBAI in New York City playing a recording of a night club routine by satirist George Carlin. The routine dealt with the "seven filthy words" that Carlin said could not be uttered on the air. The FCC set out to prove Carlin's point, and when the issue finally reached the Supreme Court, the Court ruled that Carlin's seven words were not obscene (they did not arouse prurient sexual interest), but they were still indecent. The FCC could forbid their being broadcast.

In the long and inglorious history of government interference with free speech, banning the over-the-air use of Carlin's seven words barely deserves a footnote. The general impression is, therefore, that the FCC's actions are restricted to those relatively extreme cases only libertarian troublemakers would worry about. But that is not so. In fact, the FCC's politically appointed members apparently have the power to wage a campaign against almost any broadcasting of explicitly sexual material.

In 1987, during a generally deregulation-minded administration, the FCC changed its policy from objecting to specific words used in broadcast programming to objecting to material that contained innuendo or double entendres with apparent sexual or excretory references. Having announced its new policy, the FCC then sent warning letters to radio stations KPFK-FM in Los Angeles, WYSP-FM in Philadelphia, and KCSB-FM in Santa Barbara.[12] KPFK had broadcast a play entitled "Jerker" that included explicit descriptions of sexual encounters between two men. The complaint against WYSP related to its airing of certain episodes of the Howard Stern show, one of the better known examples of shock radio. The FCC's

---

[12]KCSB-FM was operated by university students.

letter to KCSB complained about music the station had played which, according to the FCC, contained "clearly discernible, patently offensive references to sexual organs and activities as measured by contemporary standards for the broadcast medium."[13]

From a certain perspective, the FCC's extension of its powers makes sense. But even if one accepts the FCC as a necessary guardian of public decency, defining that role entirely in terms of seven specific words is little short of bizarre. We should also admit that probably nothing of lasting cultural value was lost by the FCC's bullying of radio and television stations in matters of decency, and it is possible that some children were sheltered from hearing what their parents would rather not have them hear.

Still, none of this should distract us from seeing the inherent conflict between content regulation and the spirit of the First Amendment. On the one hand, the Communications Act of 1934 says, "Nothing in this Act shall be understood or construed to give the Commission the power of censorship of radio communications . . . and no regulation or condition shall be promulgated or fixed by the Commission, which shall interfere with the right of free speech." The same act provides, however, for a $10,000 fine, two years' imprisonment, and the revocation of his broadcast license for anyone whose station is guilty of broadcasting "obscene, indecent or profane language."[14] Such language is a recipe for legal arbitrariness, and self-respecting libertarians as well as adherents to the Constitution's free-speech guarantee must abhor the resulting power of a politically appointed commission to determine which innuendos can be broadcast and which cannot.

Meddling with the Spectrum: The New Excuses

If the spectrum is not a scarce natural resource requiring special government attention, and if government spectrum management has slowed the introduction of new services, then the old system should ideally just fade away. On the contrary, however, old bad arguments for centralized government control of the spectrum are being replaced by new bad arguments.

[13]This account is based on an article in *FCC Week*, April 17, 1987.

[14]These penalties were instituted in a 1948 revision of Section 326 of the Communications Act. The original version banned "obscene, indecent or profane language" from radio communication, but did not provide for penalties.

Rather than interpreting the shift to cable-based broadcasting as a reason to withdraw from broadcast regulation on the grounds that spectrum is no longer scarce, government decisionmakers (at the FCC, in particular) have been seeking new excuses to interfere with broadcast programming. The FCC reasons that broadcasting, especially television broadcasting, communicates with a power and immediacy that the printed word lacks. It is argued, therefore, that the government must protect us from the worst excesses of this powerful video medium. This argument has two intellectual advantages from the point of view of its defenders. First, it is in no way dependent on spectrum scarcity. It would not be rendered invalid even if everyone in the nation had a television channel reserved for his own use. Second, it is based on the notion that broadcasting is distinct from other forms of media in some profound way. It may thus be seen as isolating broadcasters from First Amendment considerations.

Unlike assertions concerning the scarcity of spectrum, there is some substance to the claim that broadcasting is special in its power to communicate. Visual imagery is said by cognitive scientists to be particularly suggestive, a fact recognized in the adage, "A picture is worth a thousand words." Marshall McLuhan and Bruce Powers stressed the psychological power of video communications in their book *The Global Village*.[15] McLuhan's thinking in this regard was largely intuitive, but his insights have received support from more rigorous research. There is indeed something unique—and uniquely powerful—in visual thinking.[16]

That hardly justifies the current role of government in controlling programming content, however, and it certainly does not justify a new and increased role for government, as some have suggested. Indeed, far from justifying government control, the power of visual imagery may be seen as a reason for ensuring that the government has no control of visual imagery whatever. Do we really want or need a paternalistic government to protect us from powerful images?

[15]M. McLuhan and B. R. Powers , *The Global Village* (New York: Oxford University Press, 1989).

[16]See, for example, R. M. Freidhoff and W. Benzon, *Visualization* (New York: Harry N. Abrams, 1989), pp. 12–18.

Furthermore, government control over broadcast images could provide a slippery slope down which we slide toward de facto repeal of the First Amendment. If the government, through the FCC, acquires special authority over visual imagery, why restrict that authority to broadcasting? What about motion pictures, and if moving pictures are not to be given a special preference, what about books, newspapers, and magazines? All of them contain still visual images, some very powerful.

Proponents of FCC control over broadcasting content would hasten to reply that it is not just the power of images that makes such control necessary but also the immediacy of television. The meaning of "immediacy" in this context is rather vague. It may refer to the fact that video broadcasting, whether through cable or over the airwaves, pipes the programming directly into our living rooms. Thus, television is immediately available. We do not have to dress up and drive down to the movie house to watch the show. As a matter of fact, we do not even have to watch television at all. Many American families appear to just keep the television running, providing a background to the events of the day, watching only a few minutes in every hour of video entertainment.

The omnipresence of video in American life is surely proof of the immediacy of the medium, but is it a justification for government oversight? Video's omnipresence might be viewed instead as a strong argument for government restraint. Government oversight of something that is with us for such a major portion of our lives might be taken by some to be an unnecessary invasion of privacy.

Of course, there is always the argument that it is necessary to protect the children in the community from inappropriate materials. Not long ago, the FCC voted unanimously to mount a 24-hour-per-day indecency watch over broadcasting, the supposed purpose of which was to protect children.[17]

Defenders of government oversight argue, finally, that government control is necessary because broadcast audiences are captive.[18] The term "captive" could mean many things, but it has such a strong pejorative sense that the assertion that people are captive

[17]It is worth noting that the FCC has been criticized for being far too lenient. Some people, it seems, want the commission to launch a similar 24-hour-per-day campaign to protect adults against the perils of indecency!

[18]See, for example, *Cohen* v. *California*, 403 U.S. 15 (1971).

seems to cry out for the government to do something. A captive audience in the case of television is a strange idea, but what proponents of government control seem to mean is not that the average television viewer cannot turn off the television set (though there may be some who believe television is that seductive), but rather that there are not enough choices in what to watch.

Such a claim seems to have little substance when the average local cable system provides 60 or more channels. Even more channels can be accessed by setting up a home satellite dish. If all this programming fails to please, there are thousands of movies and other programming that can be obtained on videocassettes. Of course, there might be even more choices if local governments did not issue exclusive franchises for local video distribution. If there are too few choices, government is more likely part of the problem than part of the solution.

During the Reagan years, it appeared as though the FCC under Chairman Mark Fowler was beginning to lose interest in controlling the content of broadcasting. During the 1980s, the commission loosened rules requiring broadcasters to include nonentertainment and community programming. The Fowler FCC also eliminated time and frequency limits on television commercials, allowing both more commercials and programs devoted entirely to promotional material. The commission allowed broadcasters to sponsor political debates without being subject to equal-time requirements for candidates or positions not represented, and in 1987, the FCC voted to repeal the Fairness Doctrine. Unfortunately, the action (or nonaction) of the FCC in the Reagan/Fowler era may have had more to do with the pro-business leanings of the administration than a strict adherence to laissez-faire policies.

In the final analysis, institutions are at fault, not the persons who play an active role in spectrum management and control. We should remain mistrustful of all government action to control the content of broadcasting or other forms of electronic communications, however benign their intent. Throughout history, governments have seen independent communications networks as a threat to government authority, and they have sought to control them. Governments are not paranoid in this view. Private communications networks are an enormous force countervailing the power of government.

The communications technologies now being developed will be particularly potent in counteracting centralized power for at least two reasons. First, modern electronic communications are capable of transmitting human presence to a much greater degree than in the past. Interactive communications (including interactive video communications) are now possible both in real time and in a store-and-forward mode. They will allow the establishment of power structures that are geographically dispersed and operate quite independently of government control. Second, modern communications networks are allowing interested users to tap into vast computer databases and, through the use of intelligent computer-search techniques, to ferret out publicly available facts and piece them together to form a picture of what is going on in the world that may be less than attractive to many governments. Even in the United States, the government has proposed that it be allowed to screen commercial databases and even preclude the electronic publication of certain databases, all in the name of national security.[19] Clearly the government understands the power of modern communications systems.

What to Do about Airwaves: A Proper Role for the State

In this chapter, I have argued that spectrum for radio communications is neither scarce nor a natural resource in the usual sense. I have demonstrated how centralized spectrum management has both slowed the development of services and politicized spectrum management. Finally, I have examined how the old arguments for spectrum management, which are clearly losing force in the face of technological development, have been replaced with new rationalizations for government control over broadcasting. The question is what to do about all this.

One response would be to give the government even more power. The FCC could no doubt make speedier decisions if it were not bound by administrative procedures that attempt to guard against the abuse of government power. But reducing the extent of public participation in the FCC's decisionmaking process could lead to an even greater emphasis on political connections in allocating and assigning spectrum.

Alternatively, the government could make permanent its property rights assignments to certain parts of the spectrum in certain

---

[19]I discuss this further in chapter 6.

geographic areas. Just as landowners are given title to a particular piece of real estate, spectrum owners would receive a title, allowing them to transmit at certain frequencies with specified powers from given locations. And just as landowners can buy and sell properties, spectrum owners would be allowed to buy and sell their transmission rights. The result would no doubt be speedier deployment of new services responding to consumer rather than government interests.

There is a role for the state in such a system. It is the same role the state has in the real estate market. The government should provide a court system to enforce contracts and settle disputes peacefully. This would allow spectrum owners to develop radio communications services secure in the knowledge that their signals will not be distorted or blocked by others attempting to use the same part of the spectrum. Much of the expense and delay borne by communications providers and users over the past several decades could have been avoided had the federal government simply assigned permanent spectrum rights from the beginning.

Coda: The Vulgarization of the Spectrum?

It is interesting that the opponents of a truly free broadcasting industry and of a free market for spectrum include both cultural conservatives and liberals. Both groups were strong opponents of the Fowler FCC, and both groups are still hostile to genuine deregulation. Although both groups are concerned with ensuring that what we ought to see is broadcast, there are differences between the two groups, of course. Cultural conservatives would like broadcasting to be restricted to constant reruns of "Little House on the Prairie" and other morally uplifting programming. Liberals believe taxpayers' money should fund documentaries about homelessness, lesbian nuns, or supposed environmental threats. Both sides agree that broadcasting is too important to be left to the marketplace and that somehow broadcasting is part of our national patrimony that needs to be protected by the government.

This position is, in fact, part of a more general argument that because electronic communications will have such an important impact on the future economic, cultural, political, and social vitality of the industrialized world, it is also an area into which government should pump taxpayers' money. That argument is found in a number of guises including, for example, the demand that we subsidize

82

new technologies such as HDTV and the claim that government subsidies for telecommunications services would be funding the information highways of the future. Sadly, that kind of thinking is winning growing support in both the policy and telecommunications communities. Indeed, the highways-of-the-future argument is a central plank in the Clinton/Gore technology policy, an issue to which I will turn in the next chapter.

5. The Information Infrastructure

The view that information technology is so vital to the health of the nation that it merits special attention from the state has traditionally been embodied in two areas of U.S. telecommunications policy. Content control in broadcasting is the first; the other is the doctrine of universal telephone service, discussed in chapters 2 and 3.

Both content control and the universal-service doctrine have been with us for years, but there is a growing argument that the government should play an even broader part in the information technology business. Proponents of an expanded role for government argue that just as government has sponsored, managed, and funded the development of the economic infrastructure (roads and schools, for example), so in this postindustrial Information Age, government should support the communications infrastructure.

The communications infrastructure industry is booming. "Infrastructure" has become an "in word" at telecommunications industry gatherings, and both the National Telecommunications and Information Administration (NTIA) and the Office of Technology Assessment (OTA) have published lengthy reports on what should be done to improve the communications infrastructure. There is apparently growing support for Vice President Albert Gore's position that we need to build (at taxpayers' expense) a national telecommunications superhighway—the National Research and Education Network (NREN). Unfortunately, most of the discussion and activity misses the point. The real issue is whether our communications infrastructure would be adequate without substantial government action. The main purpose of this chapter is to show that government intervention is not necessary.

Infrastructure Policy Metastasizes

In the past, government oversight, regulation, and control of communications have been reasonably focused. Sometimes the issues dealt with have been almost esoteric, as in the case of spectrum management, and sometimes federal communications policy has addressed itself to wider issues, as with FCC content control. But until recently, there was general agreement about where government interests began and ended, even when government decisionmakers concerned themselves with the communications infrastructure. For example, the goal of universal telephone service was clearly understood to be widespread basic telephone service affordable to all but the poorest Americans. Commitment to universal service may or may not have been a good policy, but the bounds of that policy were plain to see. Similarly, it is widely accepted that the federal government should support special network facilities for those in the defense and research communities as an extension of government's more general role in national education, research, and defense activities.

Today's infrastructure debate is far less focused. Discussions of universal service now include questions about whether citizens have a right to access advanced information services. In some of its versions, Vice President Gore's NREN project would reach not just universities and colleges, but kindergartens as well. Even more ambitiously, the very existence of NREN is supposed to increase national productivity and generate important technological spinoffs.

The spreading scope of the infrastructure debate can be seen from the OTA's report on the communications infrastructure.[1] The topics listed include:

- Communication and Comparative Advantage in the Business Arena
- Communication and the Democratic Process
- Communication and the Production of Culture
- Communication and the Individual
- Equitable Access to Communication Opportunities
- Communication as Social Infrastructure

It is difficult to think of anything this list overlooks. Policy initiatives covering such a wide range of topics are a far cry from the narrower considerations of traditional telecommunications policy.

[1]U.S. Congress, Office of Technology Assessment, *Critical Connections: Communications for the Future*, OTA-CIT-407 (Washington: U.S. Government Printing Office, 1990).

The burgeoning body of government literature and the spreading debate on communications infrastructure are more than matters of purely academic interest. There is a growing passion in the policy community for "doing something" about the communications infrastructure. In the Executive Summary of the OTA report, for example, there is the promising heading, "Market Vision—Communication as a Market Commodity." Unfortunately, it is subsumed under "The Need for a National Vision of the Role of Communication." That policymakers need a new vision of communications is the litmus test for the new communications infrastructuralists. Advocates of an activist government, they have in mind much more than simply updating the 1934 Communications Act.[2] When the information infrastructuralists talk and write of a new vision, they picture extended government intervention in and funding for a broad range of communications-related areas. For infrastructuralists, the words "national" and "vision" are increasingly euphemisms for "governmental" and "policy." And there is no hint that infrastructuralists consider retreat from government control an alternative to expansion in the area of communications regulation.

What Is Communications Infrastructure?

It is often difficult to get infrastructuralists to be specific about what they hope to accomplish. At the core of their goals seems to be the belief that government intervention is necessary if the telephone companies are to build networks capable of supporting a postindustrial society. When pressed for details, infrastructuralists usually cite the need to develop widespread fiber-optic networks with digital-network equipment embodying advanced communications standards and capable of supporting services such as videotex and ISDN.[3]

There are two parts to the infrastructuralists' argument. First, they insist that there must be a *national* plan; second, that government involvement is necessary to ensure the appropriate level of investment in the new communications infrastructure.

---

[2]Actually, almost everyone would agree the Communications Act needs to be updated. The question is, in what direction?

[3]ISDN stands for Integrated Services Digital Network, described more fully in the next section.

Without national coordination, infrastructuralists argue, local communications networks will be inconsistent and unable to connect with each other. Incompatible local systems would prevent the development of a nationwide infrastructure, frustrate the development of national competitiveness, create an information underclass, and generally lead to other bad things. At this point, there is no specific reference to government, just to some centralized planning authority. Infrastructuralists frequently yearn for the days before the break-up of AT&T, and they praise the role played by Nippon Telephone and Telegraph (NTT) in centrally planning Japanese telecommunications systems.

Although AT&T and NTT are both private companies, their respective governments clearly put them in the position to act as central coordinators. Until recently, NTT was a government-owned monopoly. The old AT&T, although privately owned, was operated under onerous and detailed government regulations as a government-blessed monopolist. Centralized telecommunications planning, under whatever guise it occurs, requires considerable effort by the government to both foster its creation and protect its prerogatives.

Although the first part of the infrastructuralists' argument only implies the need for government intervention, the second part is more explicit. Infrastructuralists maintain that left to themselves, the privately owned U.S. telecommunications industry will not put enough money into the infrastructure to give us the kind of communications services we need. George A. Keyworth II, Ronald Reagan's former science adviser (of all people), said of the telecommunications industry, "The newly competitive market reduces the incentive for participants to make the necessary massive new investments."[4]

The infrastructuralists are wrong on all counts. There is no reason private organizations within the telecommunications industry should not come together to create a unified information infrastructure. In fact they are doing so already. Furthermore, far from providing a potential solution for the purported telecommunications investment crisis, government policies, if anything, are the cause of that crisis. Finally, the centrally planned projects in Europe and

---

[4]Cited in Jonathan Schlefer, "Building the Information Highway," *Technology Review* 94, no. 2 (February/March 1991): 5.

Japan that the infrastructuralists would have us copy have proven inadequate. Reproducing such programs could well slow the adoption of technological advances and new services in this country.

Central Planning or Private Cooperation: The ISDN Story

When you make a telephone call, send a fax, or transfer data from one computer to another, equipment throughout the network must make some common "assumptions" to make communication possible. In the world of telecommunications, these assumptions are called "standards." You can send documents from your fax machine to virtually every other fax machine in the world because the vast majority of such machines have now adopted the Group III standard developed by the Consultative Committee for International Telephony and Telegraphy (CCITT).

Not all communications standards are as widely promulgated. The basic standard for a high-speed digital telephone trunk in North America and Japan, for example, is the T1 standard, originally set by (and for) the Bell system. It specifies a data rate of 1.5 Mbps and establishes various other technical standards that have to do with how the information is structured when it is sent across the network. The Europeans and South Americans have a similar digital trunk standard, but it operates at 2.0 Mbps.

Infrastructuralists stress the importance of widely accepted standards, and they are right to do so. Networks that adopt different standards can be interconnected but often only at considerable expense. Nor is it just a matter of interconnectability. Where communications standards are widely adopted, standardized components, terminals, and network equipment can be mass-produced, reducing the cost of those items and promoting further penetration of the standards. Thus, widely recognized communications standards provide a homogeneous communications environment, making it easier for advanced services to develop and spread at a reasonable cost. About that much virtually everyone agrees.

There is less agreement about who should set the standards and what those standards should be. The infrastructuralists claim (in fact they all but assume) that there must be some kind of central body passing standards down from on high. Although infrastructuralists seem to prefer a direct governmental solution, a privatized national telecommunications authority would probably be considered a close second. As to what standards the central planning authority should promulgate, many infrastructuralists clearly favor the Integrated Services Digital Network.

Despite its name, ISDN is not a network as such, but rather a set of international standards being adopted by the world's telephone companies and telecommunications authorities. ISDN will allow these organizations to convert their voice-oriented analog telephone networks into digital networks capable of carrying voice, data, and image traffic. ISDN will be implemented in two phases. The first phase, known as narrowband ISDN (N-ISDN), is essentially evolutionary and will operate over existing copper cabling. N-ISDN is already with us today, and commercial services are being offered over N-ISDN–compatible networks. Simultaneous voice and data or low-quality videoconferencing can be implemented over N-ISDN. The second phase of ISDN development, known as broadband ISDN (B-ISDN), will need widespread fiber-optic cabling. When it is in place, B-ISDN will allow us to shift video information around with the same facility that voice information travels on the public network today. Because B-ISDN requires revolutionary new switching and transmission technologies as well as extensive recabling, it will not become a reality until the mid-1990s and will not be widespread until well into the 21st century.[5]

Because it seems to promise so much, ISDN has been lauded by both the policy community and the telephone industry. Commentators in the policy community seem to see in it the solution to all communications ills. There is even a book suggesting that the worldwide implementation of ISDN will lead to increased human freedom.[6] Although ISDN is immensely important, that might be expecting too much; after all, it is only a set of communications standards.

Be that as it may, all the major local and long-distance telephone companies in the United States have put large amounts of time and money into deploying services based on ISDN standards. Many of them address real needs at a quite common-sense level. Rather than install special cabling to connect computers within a building

[5]For a detailed discussion of the economics and technology of broadband networking, see Lawrence D. Gasman, *Broadband Networking* (New York: Van Nostrand Reinhold, forthcoming).

[6]Leonard R. Sussman, *Power, The Press & Technology of Freedom: The Coming Age of ISDN* (New York: Freedom House, 1989).

(a costly process both in initial installation and on-going maintenance), for example, the adoption of ISDN standards in the public telephone network can enable users to achieve the same effect by simply plugging their computers into a standard telephone jack.

As ISDN spreads, enhanced services will become more widely available. It holds out hope to those who would like to send photographs or other fairly high-resolution images over a fax machine. High-resolution fax machines are commercially available, but they usually require special high-bandwidth private lines to connect them. As a result, they have generally been used only between offices of a single organization. An ISDN-based telephone network would allow high-resolution fax machines to be used for interorganizational communications in the same way that regular fax machines are currently used. The spread of ISDN will also bring down the cost of videoconferencing by, once again, eliminating the need for expensive private lines. For those who are less interested in image communications, ISDN will add a whole new range of standard features to regular voice communications. As a matter of course, all telephone subscribers will get two lines, and caller ID will become a standard feature.

This is not a technical book, so I do not propose to explain how ISDN would work its magic, but even this short discussion of the potential of ISDN should be enough to explain infrastructuralists' and policymakers' excitement. A few years ago, when ISDN was first introduced in the United States, the resulting enthusiasm led some wits to remark that for the telephone companies ISDN really meant *I Smell Dollars Now*.

As we enter the mid-1990s, however, ISDN is still not a commercial success, and the wits are now saying that ISDN is short for *I Still Don't KNow*. No hard data are available, but estimates are that only a few hundred thousand U.S. telephone lines use the ISDN standard. Given that there are approximately 140 million telephone lines currently installed in this country, that is not a particularly impressive performance. If we accept that the United States will develop an advanced communications infrastructure, then as a practical matter, ISDN standards will have to be implemented, raising questions about its slow deployment to date.

Many observers argue that the telephone companies made a mistake in pricing ISDN-based services as premium business services. People who hold to this theory believe that such services should have been priced low to attract the maximum number of subscribers. If ISDN-based services are to replace today's basic services, it is argued, then they ought to be priced as basic services. It is also true that the narrowband ISDN available today should be seen less as an end in itself and more as a step on the road to broadband ISDN, which has huge commercial potential. Infrastructuralists are basically uninterested in these points of view, however. They argue that ISDN has failed because of a lack of central planning.

In a 1991 editorial, Jonathan Schlefer, a senior editor for *Technology Review*, defended the view that ISDN is essential for an advanced communications infrastructure, but that it will not succeed without central planning. Schlefer's message was clearly summarized in a quote highlighted in boldface, large italics: "We need a national plan [to build the information highway] not entrepreneurial competition."[7]

Schlefer's argument (which is, by the way, identical to Vice President Gore's position) is that America's economic future hangs on whether or not we rapidly deploy an advanced communications infrastructure to replace today's telephone network. Schlefer calls this infrastructure an "information highway." He is convinced that just as our prosperity in the industrial age depended on building highways across the United States, so our postindustrial prosperity will depend on building an advanced communications network.

Schlefer, quite correctly in my opinion, views ISDN as being an important paving stone for the information highway. He is less astute, however, when he blames the failure of ISDN (assuming it has failed) on the decentralized nature of the U.S. public telephone networks. Pining for the days of the old Bell system monopoly, he writes, "We now have seven regional phone monopolies. . . . The results are predictable. While the old Bell would have set national standards for ISDN, the regional phone companies each have different versions." Schlefer sees diversity as a source of weakness and calls for a centralized authority to enforce ISDN implementation from on high.

Schlefer's point is strongly overstated. To the uninitiated, his statement makes it sound as though the Bell companies are deploying radically incompatible ISDN networks. This is simply not so.

[7]Schlefer, p. 5. *Technology Review* is generally sympathetic to industrial policy.

The incompatibilities that do exist have arisen, not so much because of the Bell companies' waywardness, but rather because not all ISDN standards have been fully developed. That is not surprising. The process of developing telecommunications standards is highly complex. It consists of providing functional descriptions of every network component at every level of the network from the most detailed aspects of electrical interconnections in wall jacks right up to exactly what kind of services can be provided on an ISDN-compatible network. This is a mammoth task, complicated further by the need to keep standards current with the new technology. There are frequent adaptations and changes. No doubt the authors of ISDN standards feel a kinship to the stage character who lamented "Standards always are out of date. That is what makes them standards."[8]

In this climate of uncertainty, equipment vendors have had to develop their own proprietary standards, which have varied somewhat from vendor to vendor. As bits of ISDN have been finalized, the standards have been incorporated by equipment manufacturers into their products, but until 1992 or so too little of the ISDN standard set had been defined for all ISDN equipment to work together. An ISDN phone that worked with an AT&T switch might not work with a switch from Northern Telecom, Fujitsu, or Siemens. This problem has now been resolved, but standards for a national ISDN are still in the making, as discussed below.

A monopolistic private carrier or a state telecommunications authority could not have speeded up the development of standards, but it certainly could have imposed its will and ensured that all ISDN equipment installed in a national network was entirely compatible. Such a centralized approach is by no means necessary, however. As is so often the case, Adam Smith's ubiquitous invisible hand can do the job as well.

ISDN-equipment makers have been cooperating for some time, in fact. In the earliest days of ISDN in the United States, AT&T and Northern Telecom, the two main public telephone exchange manufacturers, worked extensively with terminal and handset manufacturers to ensure that their products worked properly with

[8]"Headmaster" in Alan Bennett, *Forty Years On*, 1968, cited in *The Penguin Dictionary of Modern Humorous Quotations*, comp. Fred Metcalf (New York: Viking Penguin, 1987), p. 241.

the main exchange. Their efforts have now been superseded by a larger effort to standardize ISDN at a national level. This effort, dubbed National ISDN 1, is centralized in the sense that any national effort must be, but it is not centrally imposed. Compliance is voluntary and born of mutual self-interest.

Bell Communications Research, popularly known as Bellcore, is largely responsible for developing National ISDN 1. After the old Bell system was broken up, it was agreed that the regional Bell operating companies needed a central services organization that could coordinate their efforts in a national emergency. Bellcore grew from that concern. It is jointly owned by the seven Bell operating companies and has become much more than just a central services organization. In addition to being an important research and development organization, Bellcore has emerged as one of the leading national organizations setting standards for public telecommunications.

Although it is a creature of the Bell holding companies, Bellcore has enormous authority in the telecommunications community. AT&T, Northern Telecom, and Siemens are all building telephone exchanges that comply with National ISDN 1. Digital Equipment Corporation and IBM, the two largest computer manufacturers in the world, have announced that their terminal equipment will follow the National ISDN 1 procedures. By the end of 1994, a national network embodying National ISDN 1 should be in place, although it might not be immediately accessible from all locations in the United States.

AT&T, Northern Telecom, and IBM have not been told by the federal government to follow Bellcore's lead. Bellcore exercises no coercive power over telecommunications equipment manufacturers. No one is being forced to cooperate. They are all responding to economic self-interest. Because the regional Bell operating companies will comply with Bellcore's suggested standards, manufacturers who want to supply equipment to the Bell companies or their customers need to comply with National ISDN 1 as well. Furthermore, telecommunications vendors and carriers recognize that agreement on some single standard is the necessary first step toward developing a market for ISDN equipment and service. Telecommunications companies do not need politicians to tell them this, nor do they need government policymakers to set standards.

Private companies can and (in the absence of undue interference) will establish and adopt the requisite standards themselves, not as a national duty, but because they can make money that way.

There is nothing unique about the ISDN standardization story. I have chosen it only because policymakers in the United States, Europe, and Japan have often appeared to have ISDN on the brain.[9] While government officials continue to talk about the need for standards, Bellcore is providing them. For example, most of the Bell companies are now providing a new service called the Switched Multimegabit Data Service (SMDS), developed and standardized by Bellcore. SMDS provides a very high-speed data service for connecting large computers and local area networks on a dial-up basis. Before SMDS, if you needed to transmit data at the speeds SMDS can offer (currently up to 45 Mbps), you had to lease a private line between the two points. With SMDS in place, you can dial up a high-speed data channel much as you would dial a normal telephone call.

All the facts are not yet in on SMDS, but the evidence suggests that it will be a successful service. Moderately sized users that need high data rates on an occasional basis, such as universities, are especially interested. In fact, SMDS will offer many of the features promised by NREN, beloved of the infrastructuralists. While the future of the government-funded NREN is bogged down in committees, however, the telephone companies will be offering SMDS.

Bellcore is not the only private group active in providing industry-wide standards. Bellcore's SMDS standard borrows part of another standard set by the Institute of Electrical and Electronic Engineers (IEEE), a voluntary professional organization that has (among its other accomplishments) defined most of today's standards for local computer networking. Here again, the IEEE enjoyed the cooperation of all the major computer and communications vendors, including the notoriously standoffish IBM. No government involvement has been required to develop or promulgate computer networking standards. In fact, cooperation between standards-setting bodies is

[9]Policymakers in telecommunications typically have a legal background and know relatively little about technology. To make up for their deficiency, they tend to fixate on a handful of technologies that are then elevated to a level of absurd importance. Policymakers' attitudes towards both ISDN and fiber optics reflect this phenomenon.

increasing. Today, discussions between groups working in similar areas are quite common.

All in all, the government plays a negligible role in telecommunications standards setting in this country. Unlike the situation in other countries where national standards organizations are state-run bodies, the American National Standards Institute (ANSI) has always eschewed government involvement in its affairs. Faced with the vast task of standardizing an almost endless variety of industrial and consumer products, ANSI parcels out the task to "accredited committees" that are frequently managed by trade associations. In the world of information technology, two of these accredited committees are particularly important. The T1 committee, which develops important standards for public telecommunications, is managed by the Exchange Carriers Standards Association (ECSA). The X3 committee, which develops computer standards, is managed by the Computer and Business Equipment Manufacturers Association (CBEMA). Both T1 and X3 have been (and continue to be) sources of important information technology standards that are copied and adopted by the rest of the world. Curiously (or perhaps not so curiously) T1 and X3 standards seem to have been especially welcome in those countries where the government spends a considerable amount of time attempting to "do something" about the communications infrastructure.

Why We Don't Need a Central Telecommunications Planning Authority

A centralized authority with the power to impose telecommunications standards from above is not just unnecessary to the development of a reasonably homogeneous communications infrastructure. The messy, slightly uncoordinated standards-making process that goes on in the United States is advantageous precisely because it results in communications standards through which different kinds of communications and different pieces of equipment from different vendors can freely intermingle. The process involved is not as tidy as the infrastructuralists would like, but it works.

In fact, a centralized approach to standardization is actually harmful, despite the claims of the infrastructuralists. They believe, and they have apparently convinced many politicians and most of the media, that the Europeans and Japanese are ahead of us in developing an advanced communications infrastructure. This lead is presumably due to centralized, authoritarian planning regimes. In his *Technology Review* editorial, Jonathan Schlefer wrote:

> Recognizing the broad social and economic effects of communications, most advanced nations have devised a coherent plan to build an advanced system. In Japan, Nippon Telegraph and Telephone (NTT) . . . plans to spend a sum variously estimated at $100 billion to $250 billion installing digital fiber-optic lines. For a decade, France Telecom has subsidized its Minitel [videotex] system. While it used to take longer to place a phone call than for a letter to reach its destination, the French now order products, do banking and gain access to databases, as well as send their notorious pornographic memos, using computer terminals.[10]

Infrastructuralists seem to believe that the very existence of a central plan is a good thing. But the real measure of success is whether a communications system, centrally directed or not, delivers the services businessmen and consumers want and need. The evidence suggests that central planning frequently leads to the misallocation of communications resources much as it leads to misallocations in most other areas of human affairs.

Telecommunications planning has always been more centralized in other countries than in the United States.[11] Outside this country, centralized quasi-governmental organizations developed and carried out communications network plans. The result has generally been communications services that are more expensive and of poorer quality than those in the United States. As a rule, citizens of other countries enjoy fewer services and suffer longer delays in receiving what services are available than do businesses and consumers in the United States.

Even the Japanese, frequently cited as models by the infrastructuralists, have little to show for years of central planning. Touch-tone phones are difficult to find outside of major cities, for example. But touch-tone capability is an essential feature of an advanced

[10]Schlefer, p. 5.

[11]Even in the old Bell system, decisionmaking was decentralized to some extent. AT&T delivered local service through 22 local operating companies.

communications infrastructure, because it provides subscribers access to a wide variety of information services. Touch-tone phones are also rare in Europe, another haven of central planning.[12]

Despite the shortcomings in centrally planned communications systems, infrastructuralists continue to advocate a more active government role in the further development of U.S. communications. Two approaches are currently being promoted. The first of them would have the government mandate in some detail exactly what services should be offered and when. The second proposal supports some form of collectivized subsidy or funding for various infrastructure projects. Once the pump is primed, advocates argue, private interests would take over, motivated by the search for profits.

The Quota Approach

The first of the two approaches has less support in the United States than in Europe, where it is an accepted way of dealing with infrastructure matters. The development of ISDN, in particular, has been subject to such "dirigism." The European Community has dictated just how many ISDN lines must be installed by the various national telecommunications authorities, for example. In most cases the quotas are being met, but the installation of the new ISDN lines in no way guarantees that they will find customers. Many of the ISDN facilities that have been built in Europe remain unused. Still, the bureaucrats in Brussels and at the national level press on. They are apparently now on the verge of mandating just how many broadband ISDN lines should be installed.

None of this is making European telecommunications authorities very happy, and they would love to find some way around mandated ISDN. Although the dictates of the Eurocrats are the law, things do not always work out as the planners would like. Consider, for example, the case of MAC television.[13]

Some time ago, the European bureaucrats insisted that all European direct broadcasting satellite (DBS) equipment (both the satellites and the dishes) adopt a color-television scheme called MAC.

[12]The only exception seems to be Scandinavia, which has a communications infrastructure that rivals or surpasses that of the United States. The Scandinavian countries have cooperated in developing their infrastructure, but they do not seem to have suffered from the fact that Denmark and Finland have relatively decentralized telecommunications networks.

[13]"MAC" stands for "Multiplexed Analogue Components."

MAC was developed in Europe, and it is supposed to improve the quality of television transmissions, although it stops short of real HDTV.[14] European authorities have foisted MAC on their populations because they see the adoption of MAC as a way of protecting European markets against satellite dish imports from the Far East.

Things have not worked out the way the bureaucrats had hoped, however. Although MAC television is European television, it is not particularly good television from a technical point of view. The enhanced picture quality is not that different from existing standards, especially since many of the program sources are fairly low-definition to begin with. In addition, MAC is not compatible with much of the existing television equipment. Adopting the MAC standard requires expensive equipment replacement, most of which will ultimately be paid for by European television viewers.

Fortunately for European consumers, the MAC story seems to have had a happy ending. When the bureaucrats insisted on MAC as a basis for European DBS, they applied the requirement only to those satellites that fall under the restrictive definition of DBS used by the International Telecommunications Union (ITU). This definition includes only very high-powered satellites that can transmit to very small dishes 12 to 18 inches across.[15] There are, of course, home-delivery systems that use lower-powered satellites and somewhat larger dishes. Many European viewers are now served by the Astra satellite run from Luxembourg with medium-powered satellites and medium-powered dishes, but without MAC.

Quasi-DBS systems, such as Astra, are compatible with existing consumer electronics, and the receiving equipment needed by consumers is cheaper than that required to receive signals from a true DBS satellite. Furthermore, because they do not have to use MAC, systems such as Astra have been free to respond to the real market needs of Europe. They have concentrated on providing more commercial television channels rather than using resources to make almost imperceptible improvements in image quality. In Europe direct-to-home broadcasting from the Astra satellite has been

[14]There is a high-definition version of MAC called HD-MAC.

[15]There is always a trade-off between the power of the satellite and the size of the home dish. True DBS satellites are very high-powered and cost a lot to build, but in theory they need only small inexpensive dishes. DBS advocates hope that the low cost of dishes will encourage large sales and widespread acceptance of DBS.

relatively popular, while MAC-based DBS ventures have failed to materialize.

Naturally, neither the oversupply of ISDN lines nor the MAC disaster has caused any rethinking in the ranks of Eurocrats. The problems, according to these policymakers, lie not with centralized decisionmaking, but with European consumers and businessmen who are too short-sighted to see the need for MAC, ISDN, and broadband communications. The bureaucrats see themselves as a sort of revolutionary vanguard, pushing the technology that Europe will need to support its infrastructure and export potential in the 21st century, while ignorant businessmen stand in the way, resisting progress.[16]

Fortunately, U.S. communications policy has avoided the more extreme forms of government meddling we find in Europe. U.S. policymakers have not set quotas for the number of ISDN lines that must be installed, nor do they usually set communications standards.[17] Still, the attitude that government bureaucrats know more about business than businessmen is alive and well in Washington. Rather than mandating the fine details of infrastructure development, however, American infrastructuralists tend to concentrate on cherry picking.

The Cherry-Picking Approach

Cherry picking requires government agents to select infrastructure projects worthy of public subsidies or special tax treatments.[18] Unlike the quota approach, which is unconnected to the market process and hence almost inevitably doomed to failure, cherry picking will sometimes lead to success. Cherry picking requires the "pickers" to indulge in strategic planning and to at least consider marketing issues. Bureaucratic cherry pickers are far less likely to come up with winners than private cherry pickers with a business interest, but some bureaucratic success will occur along with many

---

[16]In the case of MAC, such conceit is reinforced by powerful pro-MAC special interests who have all but convinced the Eurocrats that—in the name of the future European communications infrastructure—they should require MAC for quasi-DBS satellites as well as for full-powered satellites.

[17]The FCC is setting standards for HDTV transmissions for conventional television broadcasters, but so far at least, HDTV transmitted by cable operators, DBS, or the telephone companies may follow any format.

[18]Subsidies for particular projects are also widely advocated in Europe.

failures from both camps. Infrastructuralists can then light on a cherry picked by a bureaucrat and claim that it could not have been picked by a businessman.

For many, the key example of the triumph of infrastructuralism is the French Minitel project. Schlefer uses this project as an example of how government can promote the development of the communications infrastructure. In its Minitel program the French telecommunications authority (i.e., the French government) originally distributed Minitel videotex terminals as replacements for paper telephone directories. Recipients of the terminals were not charged for them, and once the terminals were in place users could look up names and addresses using a database rather than leafing through a book.

The French Minitel program has produced excitement not because of the novelty of replacing the telephone white pages with a computer terminal, but rather because once the terminals were installed other services were developed that could be accessed through them. Minitel has become widely known for its dating services and business services. There are now one million Minitel terminals installed, half of them in businesses, making Minitel by far the largest videotex network in the world. Minitel is even available in the United States. It has been demonstrated to Congress as an example of what can be done by a government determined to improve its nation's communications infrastructure.

The Minitel program does seem to have a lot going for it. After all, U.S. videotex systems such as Prodigy and CompuServe count their subscribers in the hundreds of thousands, and CompuServe has been around for a decade. The important question is, what makes Minitel work? Certainly it is not the technology. Minitel technology could be easily matched, even surpassed, in the United States. The terminals themselves are quite primitive. In fact, they were marketed as dumb terminals in the United States in the early 1980s, but without much success. The packet-switching technology on which the Minitel network is based is now all but obsolete, and in any case, it was originally developed by U.S. firms.

Minitel clearly owes its success to the government-sponsored distribution of free terminals.[19] The French government's decision

[19]Minitel is only a success if measured by the number of people who use it. It may not break even until 1998, 18 years after the service was first launched. See

to distribute terminals without charge naturally led to a large demand. As the number of consumers and businesses with terminals grew rapidly, the private sector was encouraged to develop commercial services to meet the needs of terminal owners. The hope of the French government is that the economic activity resulting from new videotex services and the development of specialized terminals will more than repay the initial government subsidy.

There is some validity to this argument. The high cost of computer terminals necessary to access videotex services is clearly one reason videotex has not taken off in the United States. Most consumers simply cannot justify the expense given the services currently available. This is a chicken-and-egg problem. Services will not develop until terminals are very cheap, and terminal providers will not go to the trouble of designing and marketing inexpensive terminals until there are services for the terminals to hook into. In France, this problem was solved by government subsidy, and for infrastructuralists, that is the only way forward. But government subsidies are not a prerequisite for developing advanced communications services.

First, there is no reason a private videotex company could not attempt to expand the market for its services by offering the necessary terminals and modems below market price.[20] Second, the price of terminals can fall (and is falling) without government interference. As the ratio of price to power in microelectronic circuitry continues to decline, the dumb terminals needed to access a videotex service will become increasingly inexpensive and commonplace. More dramatically, as home terminals come to serve an increasing number of entertainment and informational purposes—George Gilder calls them "teleputers"—the cost will be spread over more and more applications. As a result, the up-front cost for accessing a videotex network will decline substantially.

I admit that the French government should get some credit for the development of Minitel services. But credit is due not so much because of its subsidization and promotion of videotex (which is

---

Donna Pinsky, "$9 Billion Minitel," *Communications Week International*, September 2, 1991, p. 1.

[20]There is some risk that a company pursuing this course would be charged with predatory pricing. There would also be regulatory problems for any telephone company adopting this strategy.

the reason the infrastructuralists would congratulate the French government), as that it has done nothing to obstruct the development of videotex services. Sadly, the same cannot be said of the U.S. government, where antitrust laws and FCC regulations have conspired to make it almost impossible for telephone companies to make money out of videotex. It would be interesting to know whether the Bell companies have spent more running market trials for videotex or trying to persuade the government to change the rules.

Government obstruction has not been enough to kill videotex and other information services altogether. Business and dating services equivalent to those that can be obtained through Minitel are widely available in the United States over videotex services such as Prodigy and CompuServe and through private bulletin board systems. If voice services, such as 976 and 900 telephone services, are included as part of the information services market, then the United States must be considered at least as well endowed with information services as France or any other country. The United States probably has as many information services users as France when we consider voice information services accessed through phones.

Faced with evidence that the French are not so far ahead of the United States, after all, infrastructuralists continue to press their case. Businessmen may be competent to make short-term decisions, infrastructuralists concede, but they are less competent when it comes to the longer term. This is presumed to be especially true of American businessmen.

Infrastructuralists want us to be just as good as our Japanese and European competitors at planning for the long term. As evidence that we take the future as seriously as these other countries, infrastructuralists want us to emulate those countries in providing government subsidies to projects, companies, or consortia that government officials believe have a good long-term prospect. Competitive capitalism is viewed by the infrastructuralists as leading to the short-term focus of telecommunications companies and high-technology companies in general. Market competition is said to destroy the possibility for extended cooperation between companies. That belief lies behind the notion that competition reduces the incentives for market investment and behind Jonathan Schlefer's claim that "we need a national plan not entrepreneurial competition."[21]

[21]Schlefer, p. 5.

An NREN Connection in Every Home?

Such a national plan is increasingly identified with the National Research and Educational Network (NREN). Advocates of NREN envision it as an upgraded offshoot of the National Science Foundation's NSFNet. Ultimately, supporters hope that NREN will provide high-speed, real-time connections between computers at government, commercial, and academic research institutions.

NREN is part of the federal government's High Performance Computing and Communications Program (HPCC). The budget for HPCC was $802.9 million in fiscal year 1993, and its budget is expected to grow to $1 billion in four years. NREN represents $122.5 million (or 15 percent) of the fiscal year 1993 figure.[22] For the short term, NREN will be oriented toward supercomputer networking aimed at major scientific projects considered to be of national importance. These include predicting weather, climate, and global change; determining molecular, atomic, and nuclear structure; understanding turbulence, pollution dispersion, and combustion systems; and mapping the human genome.

As outlined above, not much in the NREN proposal goes beyond the government's accepted role in education, science, and defense, and I do not intend to argue with this.[23] The problem is that, although NREN may currently be aimed at the research and educational community in general and the supercomputer-user community more specifically, the long-term dream of NREN supporters is to build a national general-purpose communications network, serving the nation.

That objective is as vague as it sounds. Under pressure, NREN zealots will cite three justifications for an expansive NREN. First, other countries have (or will soon have) an equivalent network. Second, government funding of NREN will help spur the development of advanced communications technologies. Finally, NREN

[22]The remainder of the HPCC budget was applied to the Advanced Software Technology and Algorithms (ASTA) program ($346.0 million or 43 percent), the High Performance Computing Systems (HPCS) program ($178.4 million or 22 percent), and the Basic Research and Human Resources program ($156.0 million or 20 percent). *Grand Challenges 1993: High Performance Computing and Communications* (Washington: Office of Science and Technology Policy, 1993), p. 28.

[23]The entire role of government in research and education may be open to discussion, but such a discussion lies well beyond the scope of this book and the competence of its author.

will eventually lead to advanced communications services becoming available to everyone.

Keeping Up with the Joneses

The first of the infrastructuralists arguments is at the very least overstated if not simply incorrect. In fact, the United States does not lag behind the rest of the world in supercomputing networks. A 1991 General Accounting Office (GAO) report specifically determined that the U.S. led Europe and Japan in the development of high-speed computer networks for research and education.[24] This report did not faze NREN proponents, however. In fact, the report received very little publicity, even in the trade press. Had it received more attention, NREN fans would simply have responded that NREN was necessary to maintain the U.S. lead.

NREN supporters have also been unfazed by delays in other countries' efforts to build similar networks. Proponents have established 2015 as the date by which the NREN is supposed to be fully operational. That date was chosen because Japan's NTT had originally established a similar target for having in place its own high-speed fiber-optic network connecting homes and businesses and enabling the transmission of digitized voice, data, and video traffic. NTT has since abandoned its date because of the weak Japanese economy and its own falling stock price, but U.S. infrastructuralists continue to focus on the 2015 deadline.

NREN supporters argue that we must keep up with the Joneses (or the Fujimitsus) in high-performance networking to ensure that our commercial firms remain internationally competitive. It is not always clear how high-performance networks will promote international competitiveness. There are, however, several cases where government sponsorship of new technology has slowed progress.

In the 1980s, the governments of France and Germany, and to a more limited extent that of the United Kingdom, thought they could help advance their networking industry by insisting that cable-television operators install only the most advanced fiber-optic technology. The primary consequence of that policy was that very

[24]General Accounting Office, *High-Performance Computing*, GAO/IMTEC-91-69 (Washington: U.S. Government Printing Office, 1991).

few cable systems were built. In Belgium, by contrast, the government's hands-off policy with regard to cable television has resulted in a cable system to which almost all Belgian homes subscribe.

Belgian cable systems are, by all accounts, a bit behind other European systems in terms of deploying the latest technology, and that may irritate Belgian infrastructuralists, but it is apparently of little concern to Belgian television viewers. The level of technology deployed in Belgian cable television systems reflects the needs of Belgian consumers and the cost structure of the industry, not the technological dreams of bureaucrats. Many infrastructuralists' adherence to NREN and similar advanced networking projects is influenced more by considerations of national prestige than by an analysis of current or future needs of consumers and businesses or by real competitiveness issues.

Priming the Pump

Competitiveness also plays a part in the second of the three justifications for building NREN. Supporters argue that government funding for NREN will allow telecommunications equipment vendors and carriers to use NREN as a testing ground for new technologies on the road to eventual commercialization. That is, in fact, already happening. Current funding for NREN includes money for several gigabit testbeds—research networks designed to test new networking technology and applications. IBM, AT&T, GTE, Fujitsu, and many of the Bell companies are participating in the testbed projects.

The view of a government-sponsored NREN as a technological stepping stone comes straight from the Cold War. The federal government first started funding research and educational networking as a means of improving communications between dispersed researchers working for the Defense Department. These early efforts had important technological spinoffs—among them the packet-switching concept.[25] But such spinoffs were secondary to the main purpose of the early government networks—defending the nation. There is no such core purpose for the gigabit testbeds developed under the NREN effort, and while spinoffs from technology projects are often important sources of revenue, setting up a

[25]Packet switching permeates all data communications networks today, and it is expected to underpin tomorrow's advanced broadband networks.

multimillion-dollar project purely for the sake of generating spinoffs seems a somewhat convoluted strategy.

Much of the work that is being undertaken at the government-sponsored testbeds is important, but there is no reason to suppose that it would not be undertaken without government support. Indeed, participants forced to develop products under purely commercial pressures might end up with more marketable products than those developed on a not-for-profit testbed.

Spreading the Wealth

In some ways, the most worrisome justification for NREN is the third claim that some day it will reach everyone. When he was still a Senator, Vice President Gore introduced legislation that would extend access to NREN to kindergartens. On the other side of the political spectrum, Dr. Allen Bromley, President Bush's science adviser, saw in NREN the forerunner of a national network that "would be a utility, hopefully . . . supported in the private sector, that would make broadband communication available in the individual home and to the individual user."[26]

It is important to understand the dangers inherent in even proposing a national network. Such a proposal encourages a growing number of constituencies to line up for their pieces of the networking pie. Various groups—mostly from the education and library communities—are already fighting over access to NREN, and because in its start-up phases NREN involves only nominal access charges, all the new communities expect access to it as a gift from a beneficent government. Furthermore, as more groups gain access to NREN, the quality of service will deteriorate as users who do not have to pay the full cost of access crowd onto the network. Pressure to add new capacity will grow, requiring more government money.

There is another important consequence of creating a government-sponsored and subsidized national communications network: It cannot help but discourage legitimate commercial carriers with plans to set up their own national broadband networks. Why spend financial and human resources building and developing such a

---

[26]Allan Bromley quoted in Jay Habegger, "Why Is the NREN Proposal So Complicated?" *Telecommunications* 25, no. 11 (November 1991): 22. At least Bromley has some role for the private sector in his national network.

network just to have it undercut by a government-subsidized competitor? The final irony of NREN, then, is that, far from encouraging the telecommunications industry's development of new networking technology, it could prove a major brake on such efforts.

Government Collaboration in the Telecommunications Industry and Some Views on RACE

It is rather ironic that the infrastructuralists charge capitalism with failing to make enough massive investments or to respond aggressively enough to foreign competition. Even a relatively casual examination of the infrastructuralists' assertions raises questions about how serious their claims really are. Take for example the argument that competitive companies will not cooperate unless brought together by the government or one of its agencies.[27]

As we have seen, telecommunications companies have cooperated quite readily in private standards groups for many years. Even AT&T and IBM, two companies the media has seen as locked in mortal combat, have cooperated more than once—on components for a very fast local computer network called the "Fiber Distributed Data Interface" (FDDI), for example. Hewlett-Packard and Siemens have also agreed to produce the same transceiver product for the FDDI. Meanwhile, IBM and Apple Computer are teaming up to develop multimedia computing products. The complexity of today's networking technology requires a multitude of talents to bring products to market, and it has become very common for competitors to team up to develop and promote specific technologies or standards.

Although some of these alliances are focused on specific projects lasting just a few months, many are long-term strategic relationships designed to promote growth and open markets for particular kinds of products over periods of years. There would no doubt be more such agreements in the telecommunications and computing industry if the government refrained from charging antitrust violations at every turn.

These intercompany arrangements are *not* grandiose strategic plans for the future, however. Nor are they plans for a "new world order" in telecommunications. Existing private intercompany

---

[27]If only the antitrust authorities had the same perspective.

108

arrangements are not what the infrastructuralists have in mind when they call for long-range planning. What the U.S. infrastructuralists would really like to see is something like the European RACE program. RACE, which stands for "Research and Development in Advanced Communications Technologies in Europe," is a European Community program with its objective defined as "Community-wide integrated broadband communications by 1995." RACE involves virtually every major European telecommunications equipment manufacturer and service provider, and in many ways, it is a very exciting project. Many leading-edge developments in broadband communications are coming out of the RACE project, and in some areas covered by RACE, Europe may even lead the United States.

But that is only part of the RACE story. RACE is a very expensive project. It is funded to the tune of 1.1 billion European Currency Units (ecus), and half of that amount is coming from European taxpayers. RACE certainly has the attention and respect of the international engineering community. Whether that alone is worth the money being spent on it is debatable. Clearly, Europeans are looking for much more. They want material benefits in the form of enhanced profitability for European companies, more high-technology exports, and future access to advanced communications services for European citizens. In short, RACE is the infrastructuralist dream-come-true—a long-term, centrally planned approach to developing the communications infrastructure of an entire continent based on cooperation between government and industry.

If RACE is as successful as European policymakers hope, the end result would be a new generation of commercially viable advanced-communications products and services. Americans would benefit from its success in many ways. New products and services would become available through trade, and U.S. businessmen working in Europe would benefit from enhanced European communications, an aspect of European business life that has frustrated Americans in Europe for decades.

Curiously, U.S. infrastructuralists see no benefits in RACE for the United States. Indeed, they believe that RACE's success would lead to our doom. If RACE succeeds, they say, American communications high-technology firms would become increasingly uncompetitive, and the communications infrastructure in the United States would fall behind that in Europe. The general tone is of a life-and-death struggle with the Europeans to build a more advanced infrastructure.

Whatever the philosophical or political underpinnings of the infrastructuralists' views on RACE, the biggest problem with those views is the assumption that RACE will succeed. No one in the infrastructuralist community ever questions that. The very fact that the Europeans are pouring money into broadband communications means they will pull ahead technologically. Infrastructuralists have little interest in whether anyone wants or needs broadband communications. Just the fact that it is available is enough to show superiority, even if the thousands of broadband ISDN lines are rarely used.

In their enthusiasm for broadband communications at any cost, infrastructuralists rarely if ever discuss the problems and risks associated with RACE or with NTT's more aggressive broadband communications projects.[28] The most important of these problems is that no one has demonstrated any real need for broadband communications of the kind envisioned by RACE and by some of the NTT programs. The vast majority of businesses do not need the kind of capacity or technology that will emerge from RACE and the NREN gigabit testbeds. Governments are using taxpayers' money to place a bet that in time a market for broadband networking will emerge. Even if it is a good bet, it is a bet nonetheless. The impression that RACE, NREN, and similar infrastructure projects are sure things is nonsense.

For that reason alone, the huge collective efforts of the Europeans and Japanese to build broadband communications systems call for some skepticism. It is useful to remember that not long ago the infrastructuralists warned of the perils that lay in wait for America as the result of Japan's Fifth Generation Project, a collective effort by Japanese computing companies to build highly intelligent computing devices. The Japanese scientists working on the project and U.S. infrastructuralist doomsayers forecast that by the early 1990s,

---

[28]Incidentally, NTT sometimes includes major U.S. telecommunications companies in the teams it puts together to help carry out research and development programs. Industrial-policy advocates view such opportunities as a plot by the Japanese to steal American technology. Of course, if U.S. companies were not included on the teams, American infrastructuralists would charge the Japanese with protectionism.

the Fifth Generation Project would lead to computers along the lines of the human-like HAL 9000 of Stanley Kubrick's *2001: A Space Odyssey*. American infrastructuralists urged the government to fund similar projects to beat back the Japanese challenge. Despite the hype, little or nothing appears to have come from the Fifth Generation Project, and the United States still leads the world in computer and artificial-intelligence technology. The fizzled threat of the Fifth Generation Project should serve as a cautionary tale when infrastructuralists spin similar doomsday stories about Japanese and European programs in high-definition television and broadband communications.

We should view with similar skepticism infrastructuralists' claims of European and, especially, Japanese intercorporate harmony in their search for broadband communications nirvana. Zen-like peace does not constantly permeate the Japanese telecommunications scene. In August 1990, for example, the *Telecom Japan Wire* reported:

> In a series of moves that has left Japanese R&D analysts mystified . . . NTT has left ATM switch makers virtually directionless by promoting ATM switching and ISDN for the next generation public network without laying out any developmental specifications for the integration of the two. This has resulted in a slowdown of R&D efforts at Fujitsu and NEC.[29]

The ATM switches are specialized switches expected to underpin broadband ISDN, so the lack of cooperation reported here has important consequences for Japanese industry's future preeminence in advanced communications technology. Although such events may not be typical, they are not wholly atypical either.

It is true that the kind of long-term perspective that lies behind RACE and some Japanese programs is seldom found in the United States. A long-term perspective may be better cultivated in organizations that do not have to worry too much about day-to-day competition or about stock prices, and interfirm collaborations are one way of downplaying short-term competition for customers or funds. It is important to remember, however, that collaborative

---

[29]*Telcom Japan Wire*, August 1990.

efforts of the kind carried out by major companies in other industrialized countries are discouraged if not expressly forbidden by U.S. antitrust laws.

U.S. antitrust laws do make some provision for collaborative research projects, but they are much less tolerant of cooperation in bringing products to market. Many of the projects being carried out overseas are concerned with the later phases of product development and commercialization, and they would probably be illegal under current U.S. antitrust laws. The possibility of antitrust action is a serious deterrent to many companies. Any law that allows the government to prosecute firms such as IBM and Microsoft for being too successful is indeed something to worry about.

Even if the antitrust laws were abandoned, however, differences in history and culture would make American firms less likely to collaborate than their counterparts overseas. The disadvantages of the relative independence of U.S. businessmen have been more than adequately described by the infrastructuralists, but the advantages are seldom discussed. The main advantage of the individualistic philosophy that permeates many high-tech firms in this country is that it gets things done. Products roll out of factories, into dealers' showrooms, and ultimately into homes and businesses. We do not form endless committees like the Europeans.[30] Nor do we dream endlessly of future decades like the Japanese.[31] Focussing on the shorter term may be a strength more often than a weakness. After all, getting new technologies into the marketplace is the best way to improve the infrastructure.

Summary

This chapter has covered quite a few issues. But communications infrastructure is now defined in the broadest possible terms, and entire books are being produced on the topic. Many of the claims and concerns featured in the communications infrastructure debate really belong in more general discussions. Concerns about an information underclass and about how a right to universal service will be

---

[30]A casual glance at the RACE annual report might suggest that the major achievement to date has been to form committees to investigate various topics in broadband communications.

[31]One Japanese company is said to have a 500-year plan.

defined in the future are properly seen as parts of more traditional distributional debates.

I have tried in this chapter to get to the core of the infrastructure debate. The key question is whether our communications infrastructure would become inadequate without substantial government action. I conclude that government attention is not only unnecessary, but that large centralized infrastructure programs can have serious problems.

Communications standards are clearly an area of growing importance in telecommunications. Widely promulgated communications standards are necessary for a unified communications infrastructure in which there is a high degree of connectivity between advanced systems and services throughout the country. The group of standards I examined most closely was ISDN, which would allow the telephone companies to eventually put in place a digital voice, data, and image network. Surely that represents an important improvement in the U.S. communications infrastructure.

The infrastructuralists say we will never get true ISDN in this country unless the telephone companies cooperate. They say the telephone companies are not cooperating, or that their efforts are not coordinated enough. Not only do I believe U.S. telephone companies are making progress on ISDN, but in Europe, where ISDN is being planned by central authorities, the result has been too many ISDN lines that are not connected to anything on the customer side. That does not seem to me to constitute a better infrastructure.

Voluntary cooperation among firms in the U.S. telecommunications industry based on mutual self-interest is, if anything, the norm, and their cooperation has led (and will continue to lead) to development of new and powerful telecommunications technologies and services. Eventually private initiative will undoubtedly produce a network offering all the broadband services infrastructuralists are so eager to produce with taxpayers' dollars. The difference is that private companies will be certain to produce services businesses and consumers want to buy.

Of course, centralized telecommunications plans sometimes do work. Minitel seems to be an example. When centrally directed projects succeed, the infrastructuralists claim them as examples of the failure of decentralized, free-market approaches. But in those countries where centralized telecommunications planning is all but taken for granted, there are also plenty of examples where planning has led to less attractive results. Where government planning dominates, communications services are usually more expensive and of poorer quality than those available in the United States. Inevitably, there are also fewer services and longer delays in hooking them up. Meanwhile, the U.S. national telecommunications system, a result of relatively decentralized planning even in the days of the old Bell system, continues to represent the standard by which other systems are judged.

Still the infrastructuralists drone on. They believe that either the government should set out in detail exactly what services should be offered and when, or there should be some form of collectivized subsidy or funding for various infrastructure projects. Fortunately, the first of these two approaches is not widely advocated in this country, but in Europe it has led, not to the improvement of the infrastructure, but rather to excess, unused ISDN lines and an archaic approach to HDTV at a time when Europeans' basic telephone service is far inferior to that in the United States.

American infrastructuralists tend to concentrate on cherry-picking infrastructure projects. Once an appropriate project such as NREN has been chosen, the government is supposed to provide the necessary financial support. Infrastructuralists promise, of course, that once the pump is primed, responsibility for the projects will shift to the private sector. Even if such programs lead to apparent success, there is no reason to believe that their success could not be replicated within a free market for telecommunications services. All it really takes for a service to be offered is an effective demand. Once the demand is there, somehow some way an entrepreneur will provide the service—assuming the government does not stand in the way.

Direct control of the telecommunications infrastructure can be shown to be pernicious, and there is evidence that the cherry-picking subsidy approach is ineffectual, but that does not stop the infrastructuralists. Their last line of defense is that although businessmen may be competent to make short-term decisions, they are incapable of developing an appropriate long-term perspective. Competitive capitalism is viewed as the villain because it leads companies to focus on what products they can profitably bring to market in a reasonable length of time.

For infrastructuralists, there is not nearly enough long-term grandiose planning in such a focus. They will no doubt continue to press for government subsidization and control of U.S. telecommunications projects by promising a communications system that will cure all society's ills. Our best defense is a clear vision of what government planning has—and has not—accomplished in other countries and a continued skepticism about what U.S. infrastructuralists will be able to accomplish here.

Having examined the shortcomings of current government policies, it is time to move on to what should replace the current regulatory environment.

6. What Is to Be Done?

All public policy should aim at two primary goals: to maximize economic efficiency, and to leave individuals as free as possible to do as they wish as long as they do not impose undue costs on others. Most of the debates over telecommunications policy focus on the first of these goals as all sides try to show that their preferred outcome will maximize (or at least optimize) economic benefit. The second goal is seldom given much thought, possibly because there are wide (and widening) philosophical differences about what constitutes freedom and what individual rights are and are not. Communications policy probably seems only marginally relevant to questions about individual freedom, but in fact it almost always bears on some First Amendment or (what is less often recognized) property-rights issue.

Current telecommunications policy falls dangerously short when measured against the goal of either economic efficiency or individual freedom. Bureaucracy and outmoded economic philosophies regularly slow the development of new telecommunications services of all types. Continued content control directly contradicts the spirit of the First Amendment. Property-rights issues are raised by the government's authority to allocate and reallocate spectrum rights and by officials' power to tell privately owned broadcast and telephone companies what they may and may not do.

These matters are becoming more urgent in the face of rapid technological change and technological convergence. The old rules no longer apply, and they are fast becoming ridiculous, leaving increasing room for abuse. Political decisionmakers typically snarl the communications markets, because they lack sufficient information about technology, understanding of market economics, or regard for property rights.

What is to be done? In the final two chapters of this book, I will defend four proposals. First, the local telephone companies, especially the Bell companies, should be deregulated. Second, the spectrum should be privatized. Third, it should be made clear that the First Amendment applies to all electronic media. Finally, the activities of government agencies that develop and carry out communications policy should be sharply circumscribed.

Those four policy proposals are not enough to reap the full benefits of the Information Age, but they are a good start. Broader policy areas that touch on telecommunications also need attention. Antitrust law stands out in this regard. Japanese and European telecommunications firms have much greater freedom to form strategic alliances and joint ventures, but rather than punishing the Japanese and Europeans for their market success, we should free our communications companies to develop and pursue their own successful strategies.

Free the Bells

In the wake of the break-up of AT&T, the regional Bell operating companies were banned from virtually every communications market except local telephone service and the yellow pages. In 1992, Harold Greene, the judge who oversees the implementation of the AT&T antitrust settlement, reluctantly permitted the Bell companies to offer information services.[1] Whatever may have inspired it, his decision was a great victory for both common sense and U.S. telephone subscribers, who may at last enjoy a wide range of interesting new services.

But there is a long way to go. The Bell companies still cannot offer long-distance service, and they remain banned from manufacturing equipment. There have been various bills in Congress to override portions of the AT&T consent decree, but all faced uphill legislative battles. The FCC has also loosened its hold on the Bell operating companies, but it is not clear that the trend will continue under a Democratic administration.

The biggest problem with the debates over what the Bell companies should and should not be allowed to do is that they ask the wrong question. The issue is not whether the Bell companies, if left to themselves, would engage in anti-competitive behavior. The important question is whether or not the Bell companies may still

---

[1]See discussion in chapter 2.

be usefully thought of as monopolies at all. In other words, are the Baby Bells still operated as government franchises?

The first question is a nonstarter because the answer is obvious. All companies, regardless of the industry in which they operate, attempt to gain an advantage over their business rivals. To ask them not to do so is more or less the same thing as asking them not to compete in the first place. The important issue is whether the Bell companies can continue to use the government's power to suppress competition.

It may be, as opponents of deregulation fear, that the Bell companies would come to dominate a number of markets if left to their own devices. Although their ultimate success is by no means guaranteed, proponents of deregulation are mistaken when they argue that the Bells would have little impact on the markets they are currently seeking to enter. Of course they would have a significant impact. They are huge companies with extensive resources. But that should not be an argument against deregulation as long as government policies no longer tilt the playing field in favor of the Bell companies.

If we really want to see the benefits of the free market work in the telecommunications industry, we must end all regulation of the Bells (and the other local telephone companies). All local telephone companies should be able to enter any lawful business they choose, inside or outside the telecommunications field. They should be able to offer any services they wish at the local, regional, national, or international level and price them however they want. Freeing the Bell companies to enter new businesses may or may not be good for the shareholders in Ameritech, Bell Atlantic, BellSouth, NYNEX, Pacific Telesis, Southwestern Bell, and US West, but it would put pressure on companies already active in those markets, and consumers are sure to benefit from the increased competition.

Just as the Bell companies should enjoy complete freedom to make their own business decisions, so should their competitors and potential competitors. Any company financially and technically capable of offering local telephone service should be free to do so. The Bell companies might invade one another's markets, or new entrants relying on the emerging wireless technologies could prove an increasingly potent competitive force in the local telephone markets. Allowing anyone who wants to take the risk to enter the local service market is vital to true deregulation. Without such freedom, the Bell companies would continue to enjoy a real monopoly in the local service market, because the government would be protecting them from competitors. As long as they retain government protection, the Bells could use their position to injure consumer interests—just as deregulation opponents argue.

There are two serious objections to complete deregulation. The first is that, given complete freedom, the Bell companies might refuse to interconnect competitors, effectively destroying the current system in which anyone can phone anyone else. The second is that their history gives the Bell companies an unfair advantage.

Competition and Interconnection

Opponents of deregulation argue that without government oversight the Bell companies would be free (and inclined) to refuse to connect their customers to competitors' local and long-distance lines. Such behavior would, of course, represent a serious and undeniable decline in the quality of telephone service, and it is possible that, given the chance, some telephone companies might choose to engage in such anti-competitive behavior.

It is very unlikely that refusal to interconnect would remain a problem for very long, if it occurred at all. Despite the fact that each telephone company would obviously prefer to sell only its own services, the telephone companies would have strong economic incentives to offer interconnection to other companies because that is clearly what consumers want. Those companies willing to offer interconnection would almost certainly win out in a competitive battle. Real estate brokers would similarly prefer to show only properties they have listed, but a firm willing to show other brokers' properties will attract more customers.

There are some precedents that should give skeptics hope that interconnection is not anathema to telephone companies. In 1992, the FCC required the local Bell networks to provide improved network access to the alternative-access carriers. Although complying made the alternative-access carriers more competitive, the Bell companies were strangely subdued (by telecommunications industry standards) in their criticisms of the requirement. Perhaps the Bell companies expected that strong alternative-access carriers would mean more revenues for themselves in the long run.[2]

[2]Free-market advocates generally greeted this move by the FCC with glee. Thus, *Reason* magazine cited the FCC decision as an "asset" on their monthly balance

Another case of industry cooperation is electronic mail. Many different companies offering separate and competitive electronic mail systems have provided gateways to other electronic mail networks. A subscriber to MCI's electronic mail service can easily send mail to subscribers of the electronic mail systems offered by Sprint or AT&T.[3] The companies offering electronic mail systems did not develop gateways to other systems out of the goodness of their hearts. They developed them because the gateways are features customers want and will buy.

It is possible, of course, that a deregulated telephone company could adopt a long-term strategic plan to force smaller, weaker competitors out of business by refusing interconnection. There is even historical precedent for this. Theodore Vale employed just such a strategy when building the Bell system. A renewal of that approach would naturally generate howls of protest from regulators, lawmakers, and consumer groups, but those who see Vale as a villain should recall that in the end the Bell monopoly was guaranteed, not by Vale's aggressive tactics, but by the government's willingness to provide AT&T with a protected franchise in exchange for the power to regulate the communications giant.

Vale ultimately turned to the government for protection because he found, as have other businessmen in the open market, that predatory behavior is not a successful strategy in the long run. Having destroyed smaller competitors by refusing to connect them, the local telephone company could raise prices and reduce service quality—but not for long. In the absence of legal or regulatory prohibitions against entry, new service providers would be attracted by the high profits available in the local telephone market. Thus, a firm adopting a predatory strategy would find itself constantly fighting upstarts seeking to gain market share by undercutting prices or offering better service.

---

sheet. *Reason*, December 1992, p. 10. I am always a little skeptical when the FCC forces carriers to do anything, but in this case the FCC was trying to undo a wrong created by a century of government-enforced Bell monopoly. Without the government franchise, the local monopoly would never have grown so strong.

[3]Interconnection of electronic mail services is facilitated by a CCITT electronic gateway standard called X.400.

Even in markets with government barriers to entry there is hope for consumers. It was AT&T's failure to provide an adequate number of leased lines for data communications customers that originally gave MCI the opportunity to enter the communications market. High prices and slow customer service on the part of the local telephone companies allowed alternative local-access carriers to provide specialized business services in major metropolitan areas throughout the United States.

Without regulation, those consumer benefits might have been available more rapidly. In fact, the competitive responses required some deregulation, some loosening of the grip government decisionmakers generally have on the communications marketplace. Deregulation cannot guarantee low prices, and it cannot guarantee that everyone will get every service. What deregulation can guarantee is a more flexible communications system that is generally responsive to consumers. But for the communications marketplace to provide an efficient mix of prices and services, deregulation must be complete.

In the telecommunications industry, the call for total deregulation remains highly controversial. Despite the advances in technology and increasing competition, further deregulation of the Bell companies is still resisted because, opponents argue, their history gives them an unfair advantage.

The Weight of History

Advocates of continued regulation claim that the local telephone companies have inherited enough ongoing benefits from the old monopolistic Bell system to justify continued regulation. Such benefits include name recognition and the Bell networks themselves. In particular, proponents of regulation claim that the Bell companies' continued dominance in local markets is largely a consequence of the government-granted monopoly they once held. Advocates of this view vigorously oppose deregulation of any kind, especially the radical deregulation proposed here, because they say that even though the Bell companies no longer enjoy the government protection they once did, they cannot yet be forgiven for the sins of the past.

It is difficult to dismiss such charges entirely. The Bell companies and AT&T have certainly benefited from the name recognition they achieved as monopolies.[4] Although slow to respond to customer demands, the old Bell system clearly provided a quality product. Some would say that in the regulated environment, there was a tendency for the Bell system to overengineer, but in what is at times a bewildering environment, many customers feel they can use Bell quality as a benchmark. Thus individual Bell companies have marketed telephone handsets manufactured by others with the label "Genuine Bell." AT&T, and to some extent the individual Bell companies, have also benefited from the saying common among communications managers, "No one ever got fired for choosing AT&T."[5]

What remains of the Bell system has also benefited from a century of experience building and developing networks and network technology. Even though much of that experience is publicly documented, important undocumented knowledge can be found in Bell engineering lore. Nor do the competitors of AT&T and the Bell companies have anything to match the intellectual might of AT&T Bell Labs and Bellcore. Those advantages are, of course, beginning to fade as Bell engineers move to non-Bell companies and as non-Bell companies acquire their own networking expertise. Indeed, it is probably fair to say that some of AT&T's long-distance competitors are technologically ahead of "Ma Bell."[6]

All companies are to some extent the product of their history, and the Bell companies are certainly the product of their monopolistic past. But if the U.S. telephone system had not developed as a government-backed monopoly, then it is unlikely that any company could have achieved the dominance enjoyed by the Bell system. Once we accept that the source of the Bells' past monopoly power was government protection of their markets, it is less clear that the

---

[4]Officially, after the Bell system was broken up, the regional holding companies got the rights to the "Bell" name and logo. Some chose to keep that link with the past—BellSouth and Bell Atlantic, for example. Others—such as US West and Pacific Telesis—struck out on their own. AT&T retained the use of "Bell" only for its marketing efforts overseas and in the name of Bell Labs (now AT&T Bell Labs).

[5]In light of some serious service outages in the AT&T network over the past few years and the high quality of service now offered by other long-distance carriers, the weight of this slogan is rapidly fading, however.

[6]Judging from available services and public statements about their plans, WilTel, Sprint, and MCI all seem to be ahead of AT&T in terms of deploying broadband services, for example.

123

way forward is continued regulation. Of course, the regulators who have surrounded the Bell companies with complex, confusing, and overlapping rules and regulations have argued that the current environment is merely transitional, and that it will be replaced by competitive forces. But leaving the regulators to oversee the transition from government control to a free market is tantamount to leaving the fox to guard the chickens. Few government officials will readily deregulate themselves out of a job.

If we really want competition to rule the communications marketplace, we should forgo transitions and simply abandon regulation in a wholesale way. We can then focus our efforts on dealing with any undesirable consequences that arise while attempting to minimize the distortions caused by intervention.

With complete deregulation, prices might rise for some types of services, especially in rural areas, but allowing those prices to rise will provide a strong incentive for telecommunications technologists to develop less expensive ways of providing service to rural communities. In the meantime, direct government subsidies might be justified in cases where rapid deregulation threatened to leave individuals or communities without basic telephone service. In the long run (and by "long run" I mean three years or so), however, virtually all customers should pay the full cost of the services they use: the idea of telecommunications services as a basic human right is on very shaky ground. I would agree that subsidies should not be phased out within a relatively short time for the sick and elderly who need telephone service as a "lifeline." But lifeline services should be means-tested, going only to those who clearly cannot afford to pay for service. I suspect that group is quite small.[7]

There are many advantages to complete deregulation. For some, the clear definition of telecommunications property rights and recognition of the Baby Bells as full-fledged private organizations is sufficient justification. But there are also other, more practical benefits.

Freeing the Bell companies completely would allow us to get on with introducing a host of new products and services. In the current

[7]The ability-to-pay issue is quite important. There are many well-off sick and (especially) elderly people. Before offering direct government subsidies for telephone service to the sick and the elderly, the potential for help from families and charities also needs to be explored.

environment, government officials spend incredible amounts of time constructing elegant theoretical models as the bases for complex deregulatory schemes. Those schemes too seldom deliver the goods in terms of new products and services, and they are symptomatic of regulators' desperation and helplessness in an era of rapid technological change that is undermining all the old assumptions.

Freeing the Bell companies would lead to the accelerated development of the information infrastructure. By allowing competitive rather than political pressures to shape the infrastructure, its development will serve real consumer and business needs. Removing government oversight would release resources now allocated to legal and political purposes and allow them to be committed to experimentation and innovation. The communications giants could focus on developing and carrying out infrastructure plans rather than committing significant time, effort, and resources to political battles and legal fights.

Freeing the regional Bell operating companies is only half the story, however. All restrictions on outside entry into the Bell's established local communications markets must also be removed. First, new firms frequently enter markets by offering new services that can also be important in developing and expanding the information infrastructure. Second, it is competition (actual or potential) that will protect consumers' interests once the regulators are gone. In fact, the Bell companies will not be operating in a truly competitive environment until there are no government restrictions on entry into the markets in which the Bells compete. The difference between a pseudo-market in which the government issues multiple franchises and an environment in which the government provides an exclusive franchise is only a matter of degree.

Market entry free from government interference has an interesting corollary. Because much of the potential competition facing the Bell companies in local markets is likely to come from various kinds of wireless communications, free entry into local communications markets also requires unrestricted access to the electromagnetic spectrum. Bell competitors must be allowed to buy and sell rights to use the spectrum as they see fit. But that implies that more deregulation is needed to establish spectrum property rights. Freeing the Bells thus leads logically to the need to free the spectrum.

Free the Spectrum

In chapter 4 we saw that much of the discussion of spectrum allocation is based on an inappropriate model of how radio communications work. Spectrum is not a scarce natural resource that needs to be hoarded and carefully allocated by government decisionmakers according to their perception of the public interest. Rather, electromagnetic radiation is a natural phenomenon that can be exploited for a myriad of communications applications as long as the users of a particular chunk of the spectrum in a particular geographical region are protected from interference arising from the actions of other users.

Government allocation of spectrum is clearly one way of minimizing or eliminating interference, but it suffers from numerous disadvantages. Government allocation is slow and unwieldy, and it cannot respond readily to real needs. If genuine competition is to develop in local telephone markets, spectrum-allocation decisions need to be made quickly, but as things stand now, it will be years before the questions of spectrum allocation that surround wireless local communications are sorted out.

Whenever a question about spectrum allocation arises, broadcasters, telephone companies, cellular-radio carriers, and satellite companies, among others all bring political pressure to bear on the FCC to make decisions that serve their particular interests. By the time the whole political mess is sorted out and the allocation made, the technology may have changed so that the decision is no longer appropriate. New compression technologies can render the decision obsolete because the service for which the spectrum is being allocated no longer needs as much bandwidth. Or new competitive services may develop, reducing the demand for the service receiving more spectrum.

To make matters worse, government officials are bound to make spectrum-allocation decisions that reflect political realities to the detriment of consumer needs. Cellular-telephone service provides a perfect example. All major urban areas are allowed two cellular carriers. The FCC's decision to provide for dual carriers is often credited to the commission's commitment to competition in selected markets, but that view is a clear example of revisionist history. The dual-carrier model adopted for cellular communications was nothing more than a political compromise. The local telephone carriers had argued that cellular service was an extension of the service they already offered local customers, so they should be granted the cellular licenses. Companies and investors who had long had a stake in providing land mobile communications services also wanted a piece of the action. By adopting a dual-carrier model, the FCC was able to say yes to both groups.

Although politically attractive, it is not at all clear that the FCC's decision has led to an optimal allocation of resources. Who can say whether the best allocation of spectrum for cellular radio would lead to two profitable carriers or three or four or even one? The current approach to frequency allocation for cellular services is still a far cry from a fully competitive market.

The need for new frequency-allocation methods has become more urgent as a result of advancing technology. It is not merely that there are new kinds of radio technologies appearing or that they are leading to the development of new radio services with which the traditional regulatory structure cannot deal. It is also that the new technologies and services are leading to a special kind of technological convergence called the "Negroponte Switch."[8] The Negroponte Switch is the phenomenon of services normally associated with cabled communications shifting to the radio spectrum and vice versa. Thus, television entertainment, once entirely carried by radio communications, now arrives in most U.S. homes through coaxial cable. In the future, the long-distance transmission of television programming, now largely the preserve of satellite carriers, will shift to fiber-optic cables. At the same time personal communications, usually associated with fixed-wire telephones, will shift to mobile radio communications. Even for fixed telephones, alternatives to the wires supplied by the local telephone companies will increasingly be found in the form of personal communications networks (PCNs).[9]

The Negroponte Switch will mean new (and in my view, insurmountable) problems for regulators. An increasingly diverse group of political interests is demanding a say in spectrum allocation. Even more important, future decisions about spectrum allocation

---

[8]The Negroponte Switch was first identified as an important phenomenon by Nicholas Negroponte, the head of MIT's Media Lab.

[9]See chapter 3.

will require regulators to guess how far, how fast, and in what manner technological change in general and the Negroponte Switch in particular will proceed. It is virtually certain that government officials will fail in this task.

A Market in Spectrum

No central planning organization, however well-intentioned, can possibly deal adequately with the changes in technology and in users wants and needs. A centrally planned system is simply too slow and rigid in its allocation of spectrum. If we are to enjoy the full benefits of the Information Age, we need a free market in spectrum. Only by allowing a market for spectrum to develop can we be sure that the Bell companies will face effective competition. Only market mechanisms can respond adequately to the vast technological changes that are taking place in all telecommunications technologies.

But only a truly free market will do. Anything short will ultimately fail to respond adequately to changes in technology. The FCC's method for awarding cellular licenses is a nod in the direction of markets, but it is still a far cry from a true free market. Cellular licenses are awarded through lotteries run by the FCC, but the lottery winner can sell his license to whomever he chooses. Owners of cellular licenses may also provide other communications services as long as they continue to provide cellular services and do not stray from the interference levels permitted in the original license. That further enhances the quasi-market nature of the cellular business, but in a true market, anyone with a transmitter could use the spectrum in any way he found profitable, assuming of course that he did not interfere with others.

What we need is a free system of transferrable spectrum rights. Given such a system, a mobile communications service provider, for example, would have deeds that described his spectrum property, including the relevant frequencies and his maximum transmission power. The spectrum owner could choose to use the spectrum for providing either mobile communications or some other service, he could hoard the spectrum, or he could sell it to another individual or company. If the spectrum owner sold his property, the buyer might be another mobile-communications carrier or it might be an entirely different kind of business—a television company, for example. Our original spectrum owner, and all subsequent spectrum owners, should be able to take any of these actions without consulting or being regulated by any government agency. The only role for government (and probably the local government at that) would be to serve as a registrar of spectrum property rights, much as the government currently records real-estate property rights.[10]

Most of the objections to creating property rights in the spectrum are easily addressed. It has been argued, for example, that a system of spectrum property rights would tend to exclude government organizations that need spectrum to provide essential services. Police, fire, ambulance services, and the military all make extensive use of radio-based mobile communications systems. One solution might be to reserve part of the spectrum for government use. The problem with that solution, however, is that if government agencies are simply given part of the spectrum, officials are likely to ask for more than they need. Some of the spectrum reserved for government use might be more efficiently deployed in the private sector.

A better approach would be to require government agencies to buy spectrum on the market just as any other service provider (or large user) would. The government already buys innumerable goods and services, including communications services, from the private market. Opponents argue that the government might be forced to pay exorbitant prices if it is forced to compete with private interests for a right to use the airwaves. Of course, one man's exorbitant price is another man's reasonable fee, but that aside, the government tends to have deeper pockets than even the largest private organizations. If experience in other markets is any guide, government agencies are more likely to crowd out private interests in the spectrum market than the other way around.[11]

Another objection raised against free spectrum markets is that, far from providing consumers with expanded choices, free markets would result in fewer consumer options. Such objections are based first on an overgenerous view of the current regulatory process, but

[10]Such a registration function could also be easily provided by a private entity, however.

[11]To digress briefly, privatizing fire, ambulance, and even many police services would largely eliminate this particular problem. Private companies would simply include the cost of spectrum for necessary radio communications in their overall cost structure.

129

they also contain other errors depending on the particular version of the objection being raised.

Some opponents claim free spectrum markets would lead to hoarding. Speculators would supposedly buy chunks of spectrum and prevent others from using them to provide needed communications services. That could certainly happen, but there is little economic incentive for hoarding spectrum. Used spectrum is not used up like oil or some other resource with potential future value. Assuming a spectrum owner did not want to sell the spectrum or use it himself, there would be little reason not to rent it to someone else. Acting otherwise would deny the spectrum owner current income while adding little future value to his asset. Furthermore, speculators in every market buy assets because they hope to eventually sell them. Spectrum speculators would presumably be looking for an opportunity to sell their rights to someone who values them highly. Finally, even if hoarding occurs, it is unlikely that spectrum would be any more scarce than it is today, given the time lags typical of the FCC's bandwidth allocation decisions.

Another version of the argument that markets will reduce choices is that if businessmen can readily divert spectrum to whatever uses promise to be most profitable, consumers will be denied essential services or have services abruptly eliminated whenever a new and more profitable use for spectrum is found. Some areas could be denied cellular service, according to this argument, if all appropriate spectrum were being used for other purposes—to provide other types of mobile communications service or television broadcasts, for example. Alternatively, cellular customers might one day find their service cut off because a new television station had acquired the relevant spectrum from the local cellular carrier.

Once again, there is some truth in this argument. Given a free-market regime, there is no guarantee that every communications service will be available in every locale. Where demand appears to be inadequate, services will not be offered, but there seems to be no terrible injustice in this. Not every community has a good Chinese restaurant or a good book store. If a local community determines that a particular type of uneconomic communications service is essential, the community could provide a specific subsidy for the service. The absence of particular services would merely reflect the real and inevitable tradeoffs that are constantly made by persons deciding where to live and work.

Nor does it follow that the creation of a spectrum market would inevitably deprive rural America of telecommunications services. The price of spectrum in any particular area would reflect the demand for radio communications in that area. An important determinant of demand is, of course, population. Spectrum could well turn out to be relatively inexpensive in rural areas, especially compared to the prices in more heavily populated urban markets.

Similarly, there will be cases in which old services are discontinued. But there is no reason to suppose that radio-based services would be suddenly suspended any more regularly than other types of businesses close or change locations. Service providers, especially profitable service providers, do not take lightly the decision to leave business. Just as real property is sold only when the buyer is willing to pay a premium over its value in current use, spectrum rights would be sold only when the prospective buyer valued the spectrum more highly than the current user.

Of course, high premiums for using spectrum in new ways will occur from time to time. But it would happen most often when dramatic technological changes created opportunities for providing significant new services. In such circumstances, older services could well be abandoned in the rush to free spectrum for new services, and users of the old abandoned services could be inconvenienced. But consider the alternative. Under the current system, regulators decide whether spectrum will be reallocated and if so, when. Old services stay in place, but new services never get going. Under the free-market scenario, commentators would inevitably gripe about the evils of the capitalist propensity for "creative destruction." Today, the same commentators fuss about the fact that our regulatory system is holding up the development of the national communications infrastructure.

It is likely that in the future there will be less reason to abandon services despite an intensified demand for spectrum, once again, more as a result of technological than of regulatory innovation. Increasingly valuable spectrum, especially if that spectrum is marketable, will encourage the further development of digital-compression techniques. As compression technology develops it will become possible for more owners of spectrum rights to offer their original services in a compressed format, freeing spectrum to be sold or used for other purposes. While even the most advanced computer and communications technology cannot provide an entirely free lunch, that is about as close as we can get to having our cake and eating it, too.[12]

Although many of the concerns raised by opponents of spectrum property rights are frivolous or obstructionist, or both, there are also real practical issues that must be addressed by those who favor radical reform. These practical issues center on how a spectrum market can be created and maintained. The creation of a spectrum market will permit only imperfect solutions at this late stage in the game. Almost any solution will do, however, as long as it moves resources from the government into private hands. Maintaining the market represents by far the more challenging and more important of the two issues. Success in that area is critical to the viability of the idea that spectrum can be traded just as stocks and bonds are traded.

Creating Property Rights

The first challenge in creating a spectrum market is determining how the initial owners of spectrum will be selected. Some property rights advocates favor a lottery; still others prefer an auction. I believe that where chunks of spectrum are already in use, the property rights should be vested in existing users, and where spectrum is unused, a homesteading principle should be applied.

The grandfathering of existing property rights does in some cases raise issues of fairness. Many existing spectrum rights were initially acquired through political influence that would make Lyndon Johnson blush. There are understandable questions about rewarding such tactics by now granting full property rights to valuable resources, but in many cases past injustices could only be corrected by committing more serious injustices today. Persons who used their influence to obtain initial licenses may have left the scene long ago, and current spectrum users often have invested substantial resources in obtaining access to a particular part of the spectrum. Regardless of who has initial ownership rights, however, a market

---

[12]Compression, by definition, eliminates some information. Compressed signals, in some rather ill-defined sense, are of poorer quality than uncompressed signals. As a practical matter, however, that does not matter very much in many applications, including most telephone and broadcasting applications.

for spectrum will ensure that its ultimate allocation is optimal from the perspective of consumers generally.

We might want to consider an exception to the grandfathering rule for military spectrum use. With the Cold War fast becoming a memory, there is less reason for the government to control vast amounts of spectrum to guard against hypothetical dangers that may or may not face this country in the 21st century.

The next question is what to do about currently unused spectrum. The government should be discouraged from using spectrum privatization as an excuse to raise revenues. For that reason, I find auctions less attractive than lotteries for allocating spectrum.[13] Neither method is as attractive, in my view, as simply giving spectrum to homesteaders.

The homesteading principle avoids further central allocation of spectrum, and it requires only a few rules and regulations defining how individuals and organizations can acquire rights to unused spectrum. Homesteading as a means of allocating spectrum was vigorously defended by Ayn Rand.[14] She argued that if potential users register their intent to use a portion of the spectrum and then proceed to use it, they then have a moral right to call that portion their own. That seems an adequate principle on which to base the future allocation of spectrum rights. An important advantage of the homesteading principle is that it would tend to increase the efficiency with which previously owned spectrum is used. If an entrepreneur can squeeze a spectrum use between two existing users without interfering with either, he may be able to claim that part of the spectrum as his own, a possibility that should act as a further spur to technological innovation.[15]

---

[13]Auctions are usually justified by claims that the government is acting for the public in selling spectrum, and the public should receive compensation for the sale. Neither the government nor the public as a whole (whatever that means) can legitimately claim to own unused spectrum, however. Catherine England has suggested to me that because auctions promise government revenue, they may provide an incentive for the government to disgorge more spectrum, and that would certainly be a desirable consequence.

[14]Ayn Rand, "The Property Status of Airwaves," in *Capitalism: The Unknown Ideal* (New York: Signet, 1967), pp. 122–29.

[15]Tests might be necessary to demonstrate the validity of an entrepreneur's claims that he could squeeze between two other property owners without interference.

To understand more clearly how homesteading would work, it is necessary to examine the potential ongoing operation of a market for spectrum.

Coordinating Spectrum Use

Once ownership rights have been created, property rights must be specified so that spectrum owners avoid interfering with or blocking effective transmissions by others. Such questions have generated a considerable literature over the past few decades, but much of the support for developing spectrum markets has been limited in scope. Proposals have ranged from suggesting marginal adjustments to make the current government-based allocation system work better, to supporting spectrum sales as new source of government revenue. Government officials' attitude toward the creation of spectrum markets was summed up when the National Telecommunications and Information Administration observed, "This is not to say that adoption of market principles in spectrum management would mean the abdication of regulatory oversight by the federal government."[16] Among the many reasons for the widespread resistance to the creation of fully tradeable spectrum rights, one of the more important is the difficulty in imagining how it would be done. It is widely accepted that operating a market in broadly based spectrum property rights would be virtually impossible.

Milton Mueller has argued, however, that spectrum property rights could potentially be more easily established than property rights in real estate.[17] Mueller proposes that spectrum rights be defined in terms of externalities. Externalities are, of course, events that impose significant consequences on third parties.[18] Pollution

[16]National Telecommunications and Information Administration, *U.S. Spectrum Management Policy: An Agenda for the Future*, NTIA Special Publication 91-23 (Washington: U.S. Government Printing Office, 1991). Throughout the rest of this section, I will discuss the findings of this publication in some depth. The NTIA insists that the government, through the FCC and (of course) the NTIA, must stay in ultimate control of spectrum allocation. The main concern of this report is how to do that most efficiently. The study has been very influential in the policy community, in part because it is one of the few recent widely distributed and comprehensive treatments of this question.

[17]Milton Mueller, "Reforming Telecommunications Regulation," in *Telecommunications in Crisis* (Washington: Cato Institute, 1983), pp. 57–113.

[18]Externalities can be either positive or negative. As a rule, public policy is much less concerned about controlling positive externalities (i.e., benefits) that flow to third parties from others' actions.

from a factory is a negative externality, for example, if nearby residents find they are getting sick or their property values are decreasing because of the factory's operations. Traditional market mechanisms often do not provide a means through which persons suffering harm could be compensated.

Where real estate is concerned, we have developed several ways for dealing with externalities. As Mueller points out, "Western societies have evolved complicated institutional arrangements for making judgements about permissible use of property."[19] He argues that establishing rules outlawing externalities in the spectrum should be much easier than devising similar guidelines for the use of real property, because the market for real estate "is plagued by a host of complex externalities from noise pollution to public health problems [while] in contrast, the mathematical nature of electromagnetic wave propagation gives us the ability to calculate and predict the externalities caused by the use of radio transmitters."[20]

Beginning with the need to avoid externalities, Mueller advocates a system of spectrum rights based on a frequency-coordination model. Anyone setting up a new transmitter would be responsible for ensuring that his transmissions did not produce externalities (i.e., interference) for his spectrum neighbors. This proposal shifts the emphasis from a rigid concentration on who is transmitting at what frequencies in what area to a more flexible attitude in which transmitter owners can do whatever they please as long as they do not interfere with other transmitters. Mueller sums up the situation:

> Just as the [FCC's] Part 68 rules make it possible for any certified telephone to be plugged into the public network regardless of its design or manufacturer, a flexible radio allocation would allow any type of service to be plugged into the available frequencies as long as it did not create interference.[21]

Under Mueller's scheme, the owner of a new transmitter would use information about where other transmitters are located and how they operate—information obtained from a national registry—

[19]Ibid., p. 99.

[20]Ibid.

[21]Milton Mueller, "Technical Standards: The Market and Radio Frequency Allocation," *Telecommunications Policy* 43 (March 1988): 52.

135

and the established theory of electromagnetic propagation to calculate his impact on the local electromagnetic environment. If the new transmitter would tend to interfere with an existing transmitter, the owner could negotiate with the other owner and offer to buy the existing transmitter or to take the necessary technical steps to protect the existing service (if that is feasible). Alternatively, the owner of the proposed new service could make changes that would reduce or eliminate any threat of interference with the existing service. Some new laws might be needed to facilitate the process, but much could be settled by case law, and spectrum property rights law could follow the general precedents established in real estate over the centuries.

The frequency-coordination, or homesteading, approach is attractive because it would leave the allocation and reallocation of spectrum to local property owners and allow the price mechanism to work to direct spectrum to its highest valued use. Proposing that we shift to a frequency-coordination approach will no doubt be greeted by a chorus of criticism, however; chief among the criticisms would be the argument that a frequency-coordination or homesteading approach to spectrum allocation is tantamount to anarchy. In the sense that such a system would lack central direction, it would be chaotic. Particular spectrum might end up in anyone's hands being used for almost anything. But that does not represent chaos in the usual pejorative sense of the word.[22] Carefully constructed rules and laws would ensure that any individual's use of spectrum was carefully defined and controlled.

Skeptics argue that a communications system based on private property rights enforced by avoiding interference would inevitably result in radio-based services of reduced quality. The fear is that many radio users would be unwilling or unable to register effective protests against those who interfere with their transmissions. The frequency-coordination proposal simply suggests that we treat spectrum as we treat land. If we encroach on our neighbor's land

---

[22]Incidentally, there is some evidence that in a truly anarchic situation, radio services do not collapse. In Italy, pirate radio stations have become common, and the result is increasingly diverse entertainment, not broadcasts made unintelligible by constant interference. This is an apparent example of the recognition of de facto property rights, much as an individual's settlement on and use of unclaimed lands in the last century often came to constitute a real, recognizable property right.

in a small way, he may or may not object. If we become enough of a nuisance, he will certainly object—perhaps to the extent of calling on law enforcement officers.

Just as with real estate, there is no absolute measure of quality in spectrum use. When interference becomes a nuisance will depend on the use to which the spectrum is being put. The quality of transmission required is the quality of transmission that is good enough to do the job. Radio transmission of digital data communications (over microwave links or over satellite, for example) is very susceptible to errors from interference, and individuals or groups sending such transmissions would be expected to carefully guard their spectrum space against interference. Walkie-talkie services, on the other hand, can withstand considerably more interference before they become effectively impaired. If the owner of a new transmitter decided to forge ahead despite evidence that he would create negative externalities, he could be sued.[23] Most spectrum-rights cases would probably be handled outside of court through negotiations, however, just as most real-estate disputes are.

It is not as though we have no experience with establishing property rights in spectrum. Limited property rights already exist along with an active market in them. Broadcast stations are bought and sold all the time, as are cellular telephone systems. The difference is that in the existing market, the FCC provides an oversight function. In the case of broadcast licenses, for example, spectrum rights are subject to periodic renewal, the spectrum must be used for the FCC-specified purpose, and existing rights may be traded only if the FCC approves of the person or organization obtaining the spectrum right.[24] The market for broadcast licenses is, in essence, centrally controlled.

Something a little closer to the frequency-coordination method does exist in the form of private-sector coordination groups. Such

---

[23]Yes, one cost of defining a major new set of property rights is the creation of work for lawyers—though maybe not more work than regulation and administrative procedures generate.

[24]The situation in the cellular industry is more flexible, as discussed above. In practice, the requirement that cellular licensees continue to provide cellular service, even when they are using spectrum for other purposes, may be a significant limitation. With a cellular service up and running, there is unlikely to be much room for other communications services. Of course, technical advances—such as digital cellular—could reduce this burden in the future.

private groups have arisen because the FCC requires that applicants for certain types of licenses provide technical-coordination information or evidence of prior coordination of the proposed service with existing users of the spectrum. In most cases, this coordination occurs where there is no question of mutual exclusivity. That is, the new service is not going to drive an old service out of business.

Private Land Mobile Radio Services (PLMS) provide an example of how this private coordination system works. PLMS are the walkie-talkie services used by public safety officials and in certain specialized industries such as taxi cabs. The FCC certifies private groups to coordinate individual spectrum users within the broader spectrum allocated to particular groups. For example, if a new taxicab company wants to connect individual cabs and drivers with the home office through radios, the company applies to a private-frequency coordinator. The private-frequency coordinator, who generally charges a fee for his services, recommends the most suitable frequency for the new cab company and forwards the application to the FCC. The FCC then issues the radio license to the applicant. Private-coordinating committees are monitored by the FCC.

Private-frequency coordination is also used in the allocation of microwave spectrum for common carriers and for private (corporate) point-to-point links.[25] Before obtaining a license, applicants who seek to provide the services must develop engineering specifications that will ensure that their proposed systems do not interfere with other spectrum users. Private frequency coordinators aid in this effort.

The NTIA admits that private frequency coordination, to the extent it has been used, has worked quite well.[26] The primary criticism of this system seems to be the technical legal point that the Communications Act puts spectrum management squarely in the hands of the government, so that it should not be left to the private sector. While true, that is surely an argument for changing

---

[25]Very large organizations often establish their own microwave links between major corporate locations to transmit voice and data messages. Depending on the circumstances, private connections may be less expensive than using the facilities of a public carrier. Private organizations are usually precluded from building their own fiber-optic links because they lack the necessary rights-of-way.

[26]NTIA, p. 42.

the law rather than for abandoning a system generally viewed as successful. The NTIA reports, "Most commentators support frequency coordination by private user groups or clearinghouses. They argue that an exclusive reliance on the federal government for all coordination activities is unnecessary and would only serve to make the licensing process less efficient."[27] The NTIA goes on:

> In its comments the Association of American Railroads notes that private frequency coordination groups are "highly familiar with the specialized spectrum needs of the user groups that they represent." Because of this familiarity, private frequency coordinators contend that they can provide fast, efficient, conflict-free assignments to the industry users. Comsearch states that because of their unique third-party status, private coordination groups "are in a position to provide a highly efficient and expeditious method of frequency coordination that is not usually available to either the end user or the FCC."[28]

Given the current use of private coordinating groups and support for them, frequency coordination or homesteading as a principle on which to build a spectrum market may not be as far-fetched as opponents would claim. Unfortunately, the existing system of private-frequency coordination is a far cry from the ultimate goal.

In the first place, the current system is not used very widely. PLMS and point-to-point microwave links are only niches in the entire radio spectrum business. In addition, private-frequency coordinators remain, to a large extent, merely agents of the FCC. They are, therefore, potential monopolists in the sense of being government franchisees with political rather than market power. Finally, throughout the NTIA study, the systems of spectrum coordination discussed all leave the government with an active, central role in allocating and coordinating spectrum.

There are also nonlicensed communications systems that operate without anyone in the system having to apply to the government for permission to do anything. The most familiar of these systems

[27]Ibid., p. 43.
[28]Ibid.

are those used by cordless telephones and citizen-band radios.[29] My argument is that nonlicensed spectrum use should become much more the norm.

Proposals for extending the nonlicensed use of spectrum have received some support from several groups and individuals—and extended criticism from an even larger group. In many cases, the concerns of the special interests are unmistakable. Broadcasters with established stations and a vested interest in the status quo tend to oppose spectrum property rights on the basis of interference externalities. Meanwhile groups representing engineers, who might be expected to find work clearing up private spectrum disputes, have found themselves leaning in the direction of private markets.[30] Unfortunately, the consensus remains that the FCC and the NTIA should have the final say in controlling interference by licensees.

There is plenty of resistance to the creation of a system of private spectrum rights, but the frequency-coordination approach would create a system of property rights that would be superior in almost every way to the current system of spectrum allocation. Rights owners would be free to develop new services and employ new technologies without awaiting official approval. Market entry would tend to promote innovation, and most disputes would be settled at the local level by interested property owners.[31] The development of private-property rights in broadcasting would inevitably raise questions about the continued role of the government in controlling content, however. We will not enjoy a free communications market as long as the application of the First Amendment continues to be limited.

---

[29]Cellular telephones can be bought and operated without a license, of course, but they are useless without a licensed cellular telephone company through which to receive and place calls.

[30]Surprisingly enough, some very limited support for private markets has come from both the FCC and the NTIA. The FCC employed an interference-rights approach in its UHF/Land Mobile Sharing docket, and the NTIA has suggested the experimental use of an interference-rights approach at little-used frequencies, such as those above 10 GHz.

[31]Very high-powered transmitters broadcasting over wide geographic areas would, of course, require some regional or national coordinating effort.

Reaffirming the First Amendment

Abandoning the belief that the electromagnetic spectrum is a scarce public resource should lead us not only to accept full spectrum property rights but also to forsake the idea that the government should use content controls to ensure the spectrum is used in the public interest. The constitutionality of content controls as applied to the broadcasting industry has always seemed questionable, and in the long run technological convergence will make such controls increasingly difficult to defend.

The First Amendment specifically forbids Congress from making any law that "abridge[s] the freedom of speech or of the press." While it is in the nature of pithy constitutional requirements that they should be open to multiple interpretations, the choice of words in the First Amendment is particularly unfortunate because of their specificity. It is all too easy to treat the reference to speech as meaning only speech in a public place and the reference to the press as meaning the newspaper industry.

We cannot blame the 18th-century authors of the Bill of Rights for attempting to protect "only" orators and publishers, of course: Electronic media had not even been conceived of. Nevertheless, the specific wording of the First Amendment has allowed government officials to busy themselves with protecting the public from four-letter words and portrayals of realistic sexual behavior and with ensuring that, in the name of fairness, all politically recognized views are represented on television and radio broadcasts.[32] As long as the First Amendment is interpreted literally, content controls over media developed since the 18th century will probably remain. In fact, as spectrum property rights are gradually recognized, there may well be a call for tighter government controls to ensure that these rights are not abused. Government regulation of certain industries on public-interest grounds is widely accepted, after all, and to date at least, the courts recognize no specific constitutional prohibitions against regulation of large segments of the information-technology industry. But help is on the way.

---

[32]Perhaps if the First Amendment had protected "sources of news and information" rather than "speech and the press," we might have avoided content controls. The argument from scarcity would still have guaranteed the government a role in spectrum allocation, however.

Technological convergence means that the lines between broadcasting, telephone, and publishing technology are growing increasingly blurred. Any attempt to create artificial distinctions will lead to increasingly silly consequences as the distinction that differentiates common carriers, broadcasters, and publishers from one another and that underlies today's understanding of the First Amendment becomes increasingly nonsensical.

When Is a Publisher a Broadcaster?

Imagine the world of the early 21st century. Numerous households have teleputers that provide access to information and entertainment services from a wide variety of sources over multiple networks. Consumers using them will find it increasingly difficult to determine when they are dealing with publishers and when they are obtaining information from broadcasters.

Consider newspapers, for example. The *New York Times* might take advantage of widespread teleputers to deliver newspapers directly to homes and offices over a communications network. If equipped with a laser printer, the end user could print out copy that looked much like the newspapers we see today. It seems safe to assume that both the traditionally distributed and the electronically distributed versions of the *New York Times* would be considered printed material protected under the terms of the First Amendment. Of course, few *New York Times* readers receiving the electronic version would actually print the *Times* in its entirety. Those who subscribe to the electronic *Times* are much more likely to scan the material on high-resolution screens, perhaps printing out selected articles of particular interest. Now think about how things might change.

Today's telephone networks are not capable of delivering the full copy of a regular weekday edition of the *Times* complete with photographs in anything like a reasonable time. But by the 21st century, telephone companies expect to have networks in place with more than 1,000 times the capacity of today's networks. Such networks could do much more than just deliver an electronic version of the *Times* in its current format. Instead of the still photographs we currently associate with newspapers, the editors of the *Times* might want to substitute full-motion color video sequences. They might want to annotate a story about a political speech with

142

audio excerpts from that speech. Indeed, given the flexibility of electronic media, the editors could provide regular updates of breaking stories several times a day.

This combination of audio, motion video, and still graphics all mixed together in the form of a news service should sound familiar: it bears a strong resemblance to television news. There would be some differences, of course. The *New York Times* broadband video-tex service would provide more extensive and in-depth coverage of a wider range of topics than any traditional broadcast news service. In addition, such a service would be far more interactive. Readers/viewers could flip to the topic of choice, much as we do now with hard-copy newspapers.

The differences, while important to users, hardly seem to justify First Amendment distinctions. And yet, it is not difficult to imagine that if the *Times* transformation to a multimedia broadband videotex service is slow enough, the courts would simply continue to grant the *Times* First Amendment protection. Meanwhile, unless something changed, broadcasters would continue to be subject to content control.

One of the core arguments for content control's being applied to broadcasters is that they provide a uniquely powerful message in a manner facing little competition. Thus, control advocates contend that broadcasters should not be allowed complete freedom to determine the content of the message emanating from the information gateway they control. The existence of publisher-supplied broadband videotex services would seem to undermine that argument, however. With broadband videotex in place, broadcasters would face a competitor that could match their psychological immediacy and more. Nor is it likely that broadcasters and publishers would have the field to themselves. The new technologies will also attract common carriers.

Once the common carriers, especially the regional Bell operating companies, are freed from legal restrictions on their ability to enter the electronic-publishing and information-services businesses, they can be expected to offer their own broadband information services, raising yet a different set of First Amendment issues. Common carriers are not supposed to censor the content of information flowing over their networks, but it is unclear how that requirement can be effectively applied to broadband videotex services offered by them.

Just as common carriers may begin to look more like publishers and broadcasters, publishers and broadcasters may act on occasion much like common carriers. The Public Broadcasting Service is providing a data-communications service using its leased satellite facilities, for example. Broadcasters are increasingly thinking of using fiber-optic networks for backhauling video from major news events and conferences. If future broadcasters decide to build their own fiber-optic networks, they would then be in the position to lease excess capacity to others. Broadcasters will become common carriers.

Publishers could also follow suit. Newspapers such as the *Wall Street Journal* and the *Financial Times,* with broad geographic distributions, are already printed in several locations. They have satellite networks that transmit copy from editorial offices to remote printing plants, allowing much quicker physical distribution of these newspapers. Although no publishers I know of currently use their satellite networks to provide telecommunications services to other users, it is easy to imagine such services being made available in the future. If broadcasters and common carriers are bound by fairness criteria in offering communications services, would publishers be bound by similar criteria? Could a Christian publisher refuse to offer common-carrier services to known atheists or Satanists, for example? Discussion of the full implications of technological convergence has barely begun.

Should We Change the First Amendment?

There is some question about whether technological convergence should affect the commonly accepted interpretation of the First Amendment. There are many people who argue that there is, as yet, no reason to change the way in which the First Amendment is applied, and they make a convincing case. When it comes to constitutional matters, radical change can be painful, as survivors of Prohibition can attest. It is also reasonable at this stage to ask what the fuss is about. Broadcasters, publishers, and common carriers are not likely to offer identical services any time soon. In fact, the differences in backgrounds, biases, and skills of each of these groups are likely to make their separate treatment a viable approach for some time to come.

The danger in accepting the status quo is that where clear First Amendment rules are lacking, there is the potential for government

144

abuse. Consider the case of computer services, for example. There are currently few rules regarding how the First Amendment should be applied to computer networks. As a result, the government has at times acted in what many would consider a high-handed manner. In 1987, for example, the Reagan administration sent officials from various national security agencies to the offices of several private companies offering on-line database services to demand that they restrict the access of their foreign clients to only certain databases. Mead Data received uninvited visits from representatives of the FBI, the CIA, the NSA, and the Department of Defense. In some cases federal agents even demanded lists of foreign customers.

The authority for those actions was National Security Decision Directive 145 (NSDD-145), which rather ominously established "a specific responsibility for major government resources to be used to encourage, advise and if appropriate assist the private sector to protect against exploitation of communications and automated information systems."[33] The willingness of the powers-that-be to "encourage, advise, and assist" through uninvited visits to private offices is an important reminder that even democratic governments have strong authoritarian tendencies. Fortunately, the government security officials' visits to database providers were ended by a blast of criticism from numerous individuals, companies, and organizations inside and outside the information technology industry. But until the spirit of the First Amendment is specifically extended to new services provided both by companies such as Mead Data and by traditionally regulated organizations such as telephone companies, broadcasters, and cable companies, the opportunity will remain for abusive government behavior.[34]

---

[33]Quoted in U. S. Congress, Office of Technology Assessment, *Defending Secrets, Sharing Data* (Washington: U.S. Government Printing Office, 1987), p. 138.

[34]Logically, the convergence of broadcasting, publishing, and other services only requires equal treatment of all forms of information. It does not require extension of First Amendment rights from publishing to other areas. Indeed, in 1967, Jerome Barron published an article, "Access to the Press—A New First Amendment Right," *Harvard Law Review* 80 (1967): 1641, arguing that the broadcast model of content control should be extended to newspapers on the grounds that the two were virtually indistinguishable. This argument was fortunately laid to rest in 1974 when the Supreme Court decided in *Miami Herald* v. *Tornillo* that newspapers are free to print whatever they choose.

A Property-Rights View of the First Amendment

We need a new view of the First Amendment—one that interprets the protection of speech and the press to include all resources used for originating, storing, transforming, or transmitting information. The products of those resources should also be free from government interference, whether they are electronic transmissions or hard copy on film or paper. Although I am not a constitutional scholar, it seems to me in reading the history of the First Amendment that this interpretation is consistent with what the Constitution's authors were trying to accomplish. The First Amendment's reference to freedom of the press was apparently intended to prohibit governments from shutting down newspapers or book publishers, closing or destroying printing presses, or restricting the output of printed materials in any way. Extending this interpretation to the Information Age would logically mean that "freedom of the press" prohibits the government from shutting down any information provider; closing or destroying networks, computing equipment, databases, or other information resources that originate, store, transform, or transmit information; or restricting the output of those resources in any way.

Such an approach would eliminate the tension between the First Amendment and the traditional regulatory distinctions among broadcasters, common carriers, and publishers. It would also ensure that, as complex new services are developed, the First Amendment would take clear precedence over the current public-interest concerns applied to broadcasters and common carriers. Broadcasters, common carriers, and publishers would be on a common footing. They would all be viewed as information producers with equal First Amendment protection.

This vision of the First Amendment must be grounded in a rigorous view of property rights, however. The First Amendment would then become a proscription against government constraints on the owners of information-producing resources. Without a clear connection to property rights, technological convergence will generate continuing and increasing confusion. If we do not specify exactly whose rights are being protected, conflicts are bound to arise, as is already apparent.

Consider the case of Prodigy, the consumer-oriented computer service operated by Sears and IBM. Prodigy has attempted to control the content of public electronic mail exchanges among users

146

of its service. Users have cried foul and demanded their First Amendment rights. In doing so, Prodigy users have implicitly assumed that Prodigy is a common carrier. It is as if the telephone company had censored their calls. Prodigy management views the situation quite differently. Prodigy considers itself more like a publisher than a common carrier. Thus, when Prodigy edited the mail on its service, it was only doing what every magazine or newspaper publisher does in deciding what could and could not appear in its letters column.

It is fruitless to attempt to answer the question by trying to decide whether Prodigy is more like a magazine publisher or a common carrier. Prodigy is like a magazine *and* a common carrier—and it is also different from both. But note how the ambiguities clear up when the proposed reinterpretation of the First Amendment is applied. In effect, I have suggested that those who own information resources are entitled to do as they choose with their resources. Conflicts between resource owners and their customers should be resolved primarily through contracts—and unhappy Prodigy users should look for another network. They have many such options. America OnLine, for instance, is much more freewheeling and allows conversations that would be quickly excised on Prodigy.[35] Computer bulletin boards offer something to offend everyone.

Basing an extension of the First Amendment on property rights would thus have the undeniable virtue of providing a clear-cut basis for resolving competing claims. In a world where old distinctions are fading and a new generation of computer-mediated services is beginning to attract First Amendment concerns, clarity is an important attribute. Without clear guidelines, the current ambiguities will leave us open to a situation in which every interest will inevitably claim that the spirit of the First Amendment is on its side, leaving no basis on which to decide among competing demands.

The Rights of Hackers

There is an important distinction to be made between the argument for clear and distinct First Amendment protection for new

---

[35]John Schwartz, "On-Line Lothario's Antics Prompt Debate on Cyber-Age Ethics," *Washington Post*, July 11, 1993, p. A1.

electronic communications services and the argument that government crackdowns on computer hackers constitute First Amendment violations. Hackers who break into private or government computers and steal data are in no way protected by the Constitution—beyond their rights as accused persons—nor should they be. Some hackers are just mischievous teenagers and some are relatively innocent trespassers on others' property. But some hackers are industrial or political spies, and a hacker stealing data is no different from a burglar breaking into a business or home and stealing physical property. They should be treated accordingly.

That said, it is important that safeguards be erected to prevent the government's overreacting to hacker threats. The Legion of Doom case represents an example of the potential for overreaction. In that case, a group of hackers broke into a BellSouth computer and stole information from the BellSouth network. As it happened, the information was publicly available. Any interested party could have purchased it for about $13. Spurred by BellSouth's gross overestimate of the damage done, federal investigators organized armed searches of organizations and groups only loosely associated with the Legion of Doom. Eventually, the members of the group were apprehended and punished with very stiff sentences.[36] In pursuing the Legion of Doom, government agents trampled on constitutional rights, consistently attempting to obtain information and equipment in ways inconsistent with commonly accepted notions of reasonable search and seizure. Sentences were apparently driven by a determination to set an example rather than an effort to fit the crime.

Grounding First Amendment rights solidly in property rights would lead to a much more evenhanded treatment of hackers. Under my approach, hackers could still claim that their First Amendment rights had been violated if the government prevented them from using their information-technology resources to publish particular information. But a question would immediately arise about the legitimacy of the manner by which the hackers obtained

---

[36]The government's conduct in the Legion of Doom case showed a woeful lack of knowledge on the part of investigators about almost everything having to do with computers and communications networks.

the material they wanted to publish. The situation would be analogous to the legal status of newspaper publishers. If a newspaper reporter breaks into a corporate headquarters and steals documents he then publishes, he cannot easily be prosecuted for the act of publication. He can, however, be prosecuted for illegal entry into the corporate headquarters.

Examining hacking through property-rights glasses would also provide clearer guidelines about what the government may and may not do to pursue hackers. Fourth Amendment strictures that "houses, papers [i.e., information], and effects . . . shall not be violated" should apply to hackers just as they apply to persons trespassing on real property. Armed searches of organizations only loosely associated with the Legion of Doom would seem to have violated their Fourth Amendment protections. Similarly, just as the punishment should be designed to fit the crime where other types of property are concerned, so sentences for hackers should bear a relationship to the value of the information they steal. The members of the Legion of Doom were criminals because they stole someone's property, but the information they stole was of relatively little commercial or emotional value. Their sentences should have been set accordingly.

In short, hackers should be treated like other trespassers, without any special rights or punishments. In general, government pursuits of hackers have had little to do with First Amendment issues. The one important exception stems from the fact that operators of computer bulletin boards have been prosecuted because users of their bulletin board have left messages that include stolen security passwords for various networks. If publishers of hard-copy journals printed the same information, they would be protected by the First Amendment. This situation is absurd, especially because hard-copy publishers are more likely to know what is in their journals than computer bulletin board operators are to know what is on their bulletin boards.

Privacy and Access Issues

Critics hostile to private property in principle will like little that I have proposed in this book, including the approach to the First Amendment suggested here. Nothing I can say is likely to quell their fears. Persons with more moderate opinions may have lingering doubts about making property ownership the fundamental concept underpinning our legal, regulatory, and constitutional policies toward telecommunications because of concerns about privacy and access issues.

If the resources used to provide common-carrier services are treated first and foremost as the private property of information providers, then there is some chance that information-services providers will abuse the privacy of network users or exclude groups or individuals from their networks. Under my proposals, a telephone company could listen in on the conversations of those using its facilities, unless its contract with its subscribers specified otherwise, and it could simply refuse to hook up someone who wanted telephone service. That does not necessarily mean we need special government protection from the telephone companies or from other common carriers, however.

To the contrary, it is the government's power over common carriers that leads them to permit phone taps, thus invading the privacy of users. Information-service providers offering basic transmission services would have little or no economic incentive to listen in on their customers or for that matter to deny access to persons willing to pay for information services. Indeed, the market would be a potent force mediating such matters. Because virtually everyone wants some privacy, some guarantees would probably be a standard part of any common carrier–like service. Telephone users who required stronger privacy guarantees could insist on contracts meeting their specifications. In fact, some telephone companies already provide encrypted services to meet the needs of financial services companies and defense contractors, for example. Far from making communications less secure, deregulation based on property rights combined with competition would probably add to the security options for end users.

Property rights combined with competition would almost certainly improve access to information services as well. Even granting common-carrier-service providers the right to deny access to their networks to anyone on any grounds, information markets without government-sponsored entry barriers would mean users would have other options. In the unlikely event that you were denied access to your local telephone company because of your political views, you could turn to your local radio-based personal communications network.[37]

Monopolization of Information Markets

Another concern sure to be voiced by critics of the property-rights approach is that the information market would be in danger of becoming monopolized. Opponents of deregulation predict that in a free market a few entrepreneurs would buy all the information resources, either locally or nationally, and then exclude points of view they did not like. Although that could happen without adopting a property-rights approach to the First Amendment, such an approach would facilitate monopolization, critics argue, because it endorses the rights of information-resource owners to act in an exclusionary way.[38]

On the surface, their argument may seem to make sense, but a closer look at both theory and evidence raises questions about the likelihood of such a sequence of events. In the first place, the pace of technological change and the increasing number of information outlets would make it virtually impossible for one group to dominate information services without government help. In addition, information outlets giving expression to only one set of opinions would probably prove remarkably dull and uninteresting. It is hard to say, because even where market power exists, information providers generally provide diverse opinions.

Most cities have one newspaper, and most newspapers have a particular political slant. Most newspapers also regularly carry articles and letters from persons with a different perspective, however. In some cases, people buy a newspaper or listen to talk radio specifically for the diversity of opinions represented there. Thus, the profit motive often causes information entrepreneurs to provide

---

[37]Even in a diverse market, a tiny portion of the population might find itself excluded from the telephone network altogether under a property-rights approach. This group would be made up of the hardcore hackers and saboteurs who make a habit of subverting other people's rights. Although such an exclusion may offend purist supporters of the universal-access doctrine, it is difficult to see that it would be much different from the situation in which someone who has recently declared bankruptcy finds himself refused credit by every bank in the neighborhood.

[38]Such objections are not really to monopolies per se, of course. Many advocates of this position favor government franchises. The objection is to a lack of government control over the resources in question.

a forum for opinions with which they privately disagree. The market is not, in itself, a respecter of particular political views. A regime in which information resources, including spectrum rights, can be freely traded and employed without fear of political interference is likely to generate much greater diversity of opinion than an environment in which the government controls both access to information services and their content.

That does not mean, of course, that all persons will enjoy the right to express their opinions through any communications medium they choose. Markets would also continue to encourage owners of information resources to exclude those who, in their opinion, have views generally regarded as offensive or tasteless or so far from the mainstream as to be of interest to only a few people. For most of us there is little that is attractive in seeing Ku Klux Klan members or defenders of child pornography having their say on television shows. But what about more respectable extremists—advocates of socialism or legalized prostitution or drugs or revisionist history, for example? In some cases, extreme or marginal opinions can nudge the public debate in interesting and positive directions.

In an information environment dominated by a few firms and individuals, marginal opinions tend to be pushed into equally marginal outlets. For one thing, there are not enough people interested in those opinions to support their wide dissemination. More important, owners of the big information media often find extremist opinions a nuisance. They may cause boycotts and bad publicity while doing little to boost circulation or viewership over the long run. The property-rights view of the First Amendment would alter little of this. Owners of information resources seeking mass markets would have an incentive to represent a diversity of "respectable" opinion, and that would often mean excluding more marginal opinions.

But the property-rights/free-market approach advocated here would actually go some way toward giving marginal or unpopular opinions better and more secure access. The first thing governments do to suppress opinions with which they disagree is to close down the printing presses and broadcast stations that disseminate them.[39]

---

[39]Remember the stories in chapter 4 about which political interests received broadcast licenses.

Although nothing can assure that will never happen, the extension of First Amendment rights to all forms of information resources in ways that protect the owners of the resources should make government suppression more difficult. But the advantages of free information markets do not end with legal protection of unpopular opinions. The laissez-faire approach to telecommunications policy advocated herein would also tend to encourage the development of new channels through which minority opinions might be expressed. It was deregulation that enabled cable television to cater to increasingly narrow and diverse interests. It is the unregulated nature of computer bulletin boards that has allowed them to become home to every species of minority opinion and belief. With home computers and access to a common carrier, any small group will soon be able to set up an information network carrying text, still images, and even digitized video clips. Left to itself, communications technology will open up new and ever more powerful avenues for minority opinion.

The Need for Change Now

Extending the newspaper model of the First Amendment to other information services will take on special significance in the coming technological environment. There have always been magazines, newspapers, and newsletters that catered to minority opinion. They have been left relatively free from government interference, in part because of the First Amendment and in part because they were simply unknown outside very limited communities. That situation will change radically in the information environment of the 21st century. The cost of setting up widely accessible networks will be well within the reach of the smallest special interest groups. Such powerful technology, if deployed effectively, will attract the attention and opposition of other groups who will no doubt lobby for government restraints on the information resources of minorities. If we are not to fall into an environment of information majoritarianism, we must secure First Amendment protection for new communications technologies and services.

There are several possible routes for achieving such protection. Unfortunately, all have pitfalls. A new constitutional amendment supplementing and extending the First Amendment is an attractive alternative, but new amendments to the Constitution are difficult to obtain—as they should be. Congress could rewrite the Communications Act, expressly protecting information services. Given that the Communications Act was written in 1934, before television broadcasts began, a rewrite is certainly justified. But there is nothing like the political consensus necessary to refashion U.S. communications policy from top to bottom.

That leaves a piecemeal approach. A presidential administration sympathetic to market approaches might name FCC commissioners who would push some of the proposals in this book. But the FCC cannot address the full range of First Amendment issues, and FCC decisions tend to be short-lived. In the end, the best possible approach to extending the First Amendment to new telecommunications services may be through the courts, especially the Supreme Court.

An excellent framework for this approach was provided by Jonathan Emord in his book, *Freedom, Technology and the First Amendment*. He concludes:

> If there is one lesson that the history of man's struggle for freedom of speech and press commands us to appreciate more than any other, it is that free speech and press are to reside in a protected private sphere. To ensure the unencumbered operation of the free speech and press models, the First Amendment must fulfill the essential role James Madison intended for it: it must serve as a static barrier against government regulation of communication. Moreover, to prevent this barrier from becoming porous, we must avoid limiting full First Amendment protection to the print media.[40]

More specifically, Emord proposes a "new First Amendment theory" that he calls the "preservationist perspective." This perspective has two core elements: (1) "static barriers" against government intervention and (2) "adaptive definitions" for speech and the press.

Emord's explanation of his static barriers is that they "are designed to preserve the original protections of the private sphere that were made part of the First Amendment in its formative

---

[40]Jonathan Emord, *Freedom, Technology and the First Amendment* (San Francisco: Pacific Research Institute, 1991), p. 128.

years."[41] This mirrors my own preference for giving a private-property twist to the application of the First Amendment to new communications technologies and services. Emord's adaptive definitions are meant to preserve the

> intended scope of the First Amendment's protective shield, despite the passage of time [and] designed to prevent the amendment . . . from being construed to condone precisely that intervention into a new medium that would clearly be unconstitutional were it to occur in an older print medium.[42]

Adaptive definitions are intended to ensure that the static barriers remain "impenetrable . . . despite technological evolution." Guided by such a preservationist construct of the First Amendment, the courts would certainly tend to do the right thing when faced with the constitutional paradoxes that will flow from the accelerating technological change in the communications sector.

We cannot leave everything to the courts, however, and even without rewriting the Communications Act, there must be some tacit understanding of where the government can and cannot tread when it comes to setting rules for telecommunications. In the final chapter, I will describe what I think should be the government's role in telecommunications matters.

[41]Ibid.
[42]Ibid., pp. 128–29.

7. Whither the FCC?

Although it may sound like it at times, I do not support information anarchy. The most important role of the government in telecommunications markets, as in other markets, is protecting property rights, and my discussion in chapter 6 of special hackers' rights (or rather, the lack thereof) was intended to demonstrate just how the government might go about protecting property rights. Protecting property rights in the telecommunications sector extends well beyond the hacker issue, of course. Indeed, if my suggestions for spectrum allocation and First Amendment enforcement were adopted, property rights would become central to the whole telecommunications policy debate. But even in my ideal world, telecommunications policy would not be confined to property-rights issues. The government's role in structuring the environment in which information technology will develop cannot be defined in property-rights terms alone.

There are three categories of activities related to telecommunications and information technology in which the government might play a part. First, there are those activities where government involvement is entirely unobjectionable, even desirable. Second, there are borderline cases where there is some reason to question government involvement, but practical considerations weigh on the other side. Finally, there are those activities where government involvement is simply a bad idea. The message of this book has clearly been that much—perhaps most—government activity in the communications arena falls squarely in the third category. It is unnecessary and indeed undesirable. This final chapter will explore the first and second types of government activity.

The Government as a Telecommunications User

The first category of activities—those where government activity is unobjectionable—consists of two types of activity. The most significant is the creation of a legal environment in which private property rights come to dominate in allocation and use decisions.

Because I have spent the better part of six chapters discussing that issue, especially as it relates to the creation of private rights to the spectrum, I will not pursue the matter here.

I also regard as entirely unobjectionable the government's playing the part of an active large user of telecommunications services. Even in a far more libertarian world, government would not fade away entirely, and so would continue to be a large user of communications services in fulfilling both its civil and military responsibilities. Given that, it is wholly legitimate for the government to act just as other large telecommunications users act when they set de facto standards for electronic communications of various kinds.

In fact, the government is already doing this. A set of standards called TCP/IP, which allows computing equipment from one vendor to talk to computing equipment from another vendor, grew originally from specifications for government military networks. Those standards are now widely used throughout the commercial computing and communications community.[1] The spread of those standards from military to commercial use has been a natural evolution. No one demanded that private industry adopt them. In fact, they might have been developed by any large user. The sponsors of communications industry standards are usually equipment manufacturers or large telephone companies, and nongovernment users have also been known to sponsor standards. Boeing and General Motors have each devised standards for factory automation networks, for example.

There are no political or economic reasons why the government should not specify certain standards for the telecommunications services and equipment it buys. That seems only prudent for any large procurer of telecommunications and computing products and services. If nongovernmental users find the standards of some use to them, all well and good. There is no problem as long as the government does not insist that private telecommunications users adopt its standards.

[1]TCP/IP stands for "Transport Control Protocol/Internet Protocol." It is actually two standards (TCP and IP), each with a somewhat different function, but they are almost always used together. A few years ago the consensus was that TCP/IP would eventually be replaced by the Open Systems Interconnection (OSI) standards, international standards that were in theory superior to TCP/IP. That has not occurred, although some parts of the OSI program have been quite successful. Ironically, the U.S. government has been one of the few promoters of OSI.

Its role as a large user of telecommunications equipment and services may also lead the government to join and play a significant role in the major standards organizations. That does not mean, however, that the government would be acting as an official setter of national standards, and the distinction is important. The U.S. government has always avoided a direct role in setting domestic standards. The American National Standards Institute (ANSI), which coordinates standards-setting in a wide range of industries, remains a private organization. Unfortunately, things become more complicated when we move to international communications markets.

Borderline Cases

I have identified two borderline cases where government activity, although not clearly desirable or unobjectionable, has important practical advantages. The first involves U.S. representation to international standards-setting bodies, and the second case deals with the role government agencies should play as we move toward a market-based telecommunications system.

International Telecommunications Organizations

In most other countries telecommunications at the national level is dominated by government-owned entities. As a result, the primary international telecommunications organizations generally assume that various countries' interests will be represented by their governments. The question for the United States has long been who should represent our interests in such forums.

Consider, for example, the International Telecommunications Union (ITU). The ITU is a venerable organization that began life in 1865 as the International Telegraph Union. It is now the United Nations agency responsible for

> the regulation and planning of worldwide telecommunication and the establishment of operating standards for equipment and systems, the coordination and dissemination of information required for the planning and operation of telecommunication services and the promotion of and contribution to the development of telecommunication and related services.[2]

[2]A. Macpherson, *International Telecommunication Standards Organizations* (Boston: Artech House, 1990), p. 12.

The ITU does valuable standards-setting work through its subsidiary organizations, the Consultative Committee for International Radio (CCIR) for radio and satellite communications and the Consultative Committee for International Telephony and Telegraphy (CCITT) for just about everything else. When all is said and done, however, the ITU is a club for government telecommunications monopolies, and it represents the interests of those authorities.

Fortunately, the United States has never had a government telecommunications monopoly with government employees operating the telephone system. Consequently, U.S. interests are represented at the ITU by a complex mix of government and private organizations. Representatives from the FCC and the Department of Commerce deal with regulatory matters, personnel from the Department of State address international-relations issues, and technical matters are left largely to private-sector representatives, which historically has meant AT&T engineers. The ITU's proceedings have a reputation for being slow, unwieldy, and politically charged, and a healthy dose of market discipline would no doubt go some way toward improving the situation.[3] There is little doubt, however, that the ITU provides an important international forum for setting standards.

A case in point is facsimile transmission. Individuals involved in international business now take for granted that they can send documents from one fax to another in any other part of the globe, no matter who manufactured the machines in question. But when fax first appeared, that was not the case.[4] IBM had its own standards for fax machines. If you had an IBM fax, you needed another IBM machine at the other end of the link for the document to be successfully transmitted. This situation has obviously changed— in large part because of the fax standards established by the CCITT, which has promulgated four separate fax standards over the years, all designed to enable fax machines to freely interconnect.[5] As

[3]Telecommunications journalist Carl Malamud relates how, ironically, the ITU itself uses antiquated telecommunications equipment. See Carl Malamud, *Exploring the Internet* (Englewood Cliffs, N.J.: Prentice-Hall, 1992), pp. 6–7.

[4]Facsimile is actually a very old technology. Patents for facsimile machines are at least as old as those for the telephone itself. Nevertheless, facsimile did not make it into offices until the 1970s and boomed only in the 1980s.

[5]The Group I and Group II standards are now obsolete, but there are still some functioning Group I and Group II machines around, especially outside the developed world. Virtually all the fax machines in the United States are compatible with the

far as I know, manufacturers now offer only CCITT-compatible machines.

The CCITT has recently turned its attention to videoconferencing equipment, a business in which each manufacturer still has its own standards. Until the CCITT came along with its so-called Px64 standards, someone with a videoconferencing system from Picture-Tel who wanted to run a videoconference with a location that had equipment from Compression Labs would need to buy time on an interconnecting network that could convert between the two standards. With Px64 in place, you can plug your videoconferencing system into the wall (if you have ISDN or something like it) and talk to whomever you like. Px64 delivers a picture quality inferior to the proprietary standards from the main videoconferencing equipment vendors, but things are improving.

There are many other important examples of standards that have been developed by the CCITT and the CCIR. There have also been failures—the CCIR standards for direct-to-home satellite broadcasting, for example—but no one is perfect. International standardization of the kind provided by the CCITT and the CCIR is vital to the development of international telecommunications. It is unfortunate that the CCITT, CCIR, and ITU are so heavily influenced by governments and government-controlled telecommunications authorities, but private vendors and carriers are also actively involved in decision-making at the standards forums organized by the international bodies. Furthermore, no one forces manufacturers and national telephone companies to adopt the standards set by them. New standards are frequently ignored or changed to suit existing circumstances.

The CCIR and CCITT might ultimately evolve into nonprofit groups whose members are commercial companies and major end users of telecommunications products and services rather than governments.[6] U.S. representatives to the ITU, CCIR, and CCITT

CCITT Group III standards. There is also a CCITT Group IV standard for more advanced machines found mostly in Japan. The essential difference between machines in the different groups is in the quality of their end products and the speed with which they will transmit a document. The higher the group number, the higher the quality and the faster the transmission.

[6]There are several examples of private companies working together to develop industrywide standards. Because such cooperative groups have a vested interest in having their standards adopted as widely as possible, however, the standards-setting groups tend not to care about making money, per se. Cooperative standards-setting organizations tend to be operated on a nonprofit basis, but the ultimate

should attempt to use whatever influence they have to encourage the transformation of the groups into private organizations. Unfortunately, U.S. influence in this area is limited, and U.S. cooperation with the international standards process remains essential.

The belief that U.S. government involvement in the ITU and its affiliates should continue does not fit very comfortably with many of my other conclusions, but as a practical matter it seems to be necessary. Here then is a borderline case in which continued government involvement seems to be unavoidable.

International telecommunications organizations do not include just standards-setting organizations. Among the more prominent of the international telecommunications bodies are two international satellite organizations—Intelsat and Inmarsat. As with the ITU, Intelsat and Inmarsat were designed primarily as international forums for governments' coordination efforts. Thus, the ultimate fate of most transcontinental satellite communications rests in the hands of national governments.

Intelsat was established in 1964 to provide international satellite service to the world's telecommunications authorities and broadcasters, most of which are government agencies. Inmarsat was created in the late 1970s to provide satellite communications service for vessels at sea. Inmarsat is now diversifying into the rapidly growing area of land-based mobile communications and air-to-ground communications. Both Intelsat and Inmarsat have similar organizational structures, so we will focus primarily on Intelsat.

Intelsat is governed by four administrative bodies. Two of them—the Assembly of Parties and the Board of Governors—consist specifically of government representatives. A third administrative body—the Meeting of Signatories—consists of representatives from the national telecommunications carriers. The fourth body—the Executive Organ—is made up of Intelsat employees, and it actually governs the day-to-day activities of that international organization.

Because most countries still operate their telecommunications services as government monopolies or something close, the carrier representatives at the Meeting of Signatories are government employees as a rule. The United States is one of the few countries represented by a private company. The Communications Satellite

---

reason commercial companies become involved in standards-setting activities is to improve their bottom line.

Corporation, invariably referred to as Comsat, was specifically established to serve as the U.S. representative to Intelsat.[7] But while Comsat is nominally a private company, it is also a government franchise. It is the only organization permitted to access the Intelsat satellite network from the United States. All long-distance telephone companies and broadcasters who want to use Intelsat must buy through Comsat. Comsat has the trappings of a private company, it has been involved in a variety of satellite-related commercial activities, and its stock is traded publicly, but it is far from being shaped solely by the market.

Still, the U.S. government has been an important force for change within the international telecommunications community. The United States has always allowed private companies' representatives to participate directly in international telecommunications organizations. Successive U.S. administrations have also been more sympathetic than other governments to the idea of allowing economic rather than just political forces to shape Intelsat and Inmarsat. Thus, actions by the U.S. government remain one of the best hopes for subjecting Intelsat and Inmarsat to increased market discipline.

A growing literature argues that international satellite communications organizations need to be more responsive to market forces. That is hardly surprising. Virtually all of the services offered by Intelsat and Inmarsat now face competition from rival communications networks controlled either by national governments or by private interests. Unfortunately, even U.S. support for increased reliance on market forces has too often been lukewarm. The Reagan administration took an important step forward when it permitted the establishment of private international satellite networks, an innovation that has helped force Intelsat to face market realities and started it on the road to creating new pricing strategies and service offerings.

Private satellite systems still face limits, however. They are not allowed to carry switched common-carrier-type services, and much of the more lucrative international satellite business thus remains

---

[7]AT&T might have been chosen for this task, but U.S. policymakers felt there would be a conflict of interest because AT&T is one of several competitive U.S.-based users of the Intelsat system.

closed to them.[8] In March 1992, the FCC announced that the ban would end in 1997, and until then, private satellites will be able to offer private lines interconnected to switched public services. Although still limited, that is a significant improvement on the old situation where private satellites could offer services only to isolated private networks.

In fact, the very existence of private international satellite systems undermines the legitimacy of the international satellite organizations. The raison d'être for Intelsat and Inmarsat was that private systems could not be supported by the market. But there is increasing evidence that, whatever the situation in the past, the private sector would happily support several international communications satellite systems today. The PanAmSat system has proved very successful despite the efforts of Intelsat to stack the cards against it, and there are increasing numbers of private companies eager to provide satellite-based communications services.

Ultimately, there is little reason why Intelsat and Inmarsat should not be speedily privatized. They could then offer their services directly to end users, through third parties, or in whatever way the market dictated.[9]

Some observers have argued that Intelsat and Inmarsat are already privatized in a sense. Power in both of them is based on use of the system, and some very large users—most notably the United States and the United Kingdom—are represented at Intelsat and Inmarsat by private entities (Comsat and British Telecom). But it is an exaggeration to talk of Intelsat and Inmarsat as private organizations. They cannot be considered to have been privatized until all governmental representation within them ends and all

---

[8]The restriction on switched services is curious. One could argue that to encourage competition in a market dominated by a quasi-governmental entity, new private entities should be given an advantage. The ban on offering switched services is effectively starting private entrants off with a handicap, however.

[9]Opponents of privatization point out that one function of both Inmarsat and Intelsat has been to provide "socially useful" services such as emergency services and domestic satellite services for Third World countries. Such services could probably not survive in an entirely market-driven environment. But as with emergency services within the United States, it makes more sense to subsidize them than to construct an entire global communications strategy simply on the basis that they must be provided.

regulatory barriers to entry for other private satellite carriers have been eliminated.

Such barriers to entry go beyond the restrictions on switched services. Intelsat has the authority to coordinate any international satellite system's construction to ensure that new satellite capacity does not create too much competition for Intelsat. Although Intelsat has gradually moderated its opposition to alternative international satellite systems, it is reluctant to give up its coordination authority entirely. Clearly no truly private company has government-backed authority to prevent rivals from expanding too much.

Government control of Intelsat and Inmarsat is no more welcome than government control of a domestic telephone company, and the continued involvement of the U.S. government in Intelsat, either through direct representation or through a single franchisee, is unfortunate. The problem, once again, is the limited ability of the United States to effect a change in them. Privatization appears unlikely, at least in the foreseeable future. Because Intelsat and Inmarsat are international bodies, the U.S. government cannot legislate, regulate, or set directives that will directly change their structure. Nor can the United States substitute private organizations for government representation at the higher reaches of the Intelsat and Inmarsat organizations, because government representation is specifically mandated by their charters. Similarly, Comsat cannot be replaced by competitive access to Intelsat facilities because the Intelsat charter requires that access should be either through a government-operated organization or through a franchise.

The most the U.S. government can do is attempt to influence other governments by example or through political influence, and there are limits to what the United States can accomplish with its influence. Because much of Intelsat's funding comes from this country, the U.S. government could attempt to force fundamental change at Intelsat by threatening to withdraw funding. U.S. withdrawal from Intelsat would almost certainly lead to radical changes, perhaps even in the direction of more market orientation. But the loss of access to Intelsat would be a serious blow to U.S. long-distance carriers and broadcasters. Until more private international facilities come on-line, withdrawal does not seem a very promising route. Continued U.S. participation in Intelsat and Inmarsat, therefore, appears to be another case where government involvement is, regrettably, necessary—at least for the time being.

Managing the Transition

Despite the many pitfalls for a market-oriented telecommunications policy in the international arena, at home at least, the proposals I have suggested, if they were adopted, would guarantee that government interference in telecommunications markets would ultimately be very limited. That said, the government may still need to serve a transitional role as the telecommunications industry moves from government control toward laissez faire. I write those words with some fear and trepidation. It seems to be a law of political science that once government officials are given a role, they will fight to keep it and expand it long after the reason for it has passed.

Still, abruptly abandoning all the rules, regulations, and directives that constitute today's telecommunications policy would probably lead to chaos. I have little doubt that ultimately—perhaps a year or so later—the chaos would evaporate and an organized orderly market would appear, but the transition could be very painful. Thus, as the telecommunications sector, with its tradition of ubiquitous government franchises, struggles to become a true market, we might find it necessary to monitor the emerging marketplace at least temporarily.

Allowing the government to fulfill that role is, of course, leaving the fox to look after the chickens, but there may be relatively little choice in the matter. The personnel best able to monitor the emerging market are probably at the FCC.[10] The challenge is to devise and put in place safeguards that will ensure that interim arrangements for monitoring the progress of the emerging telecommunications market do not become self-perpetuating.

First, persons charged with the task of overseeing the deregulation of the telecommunications market should not come entirely from the ranks of existing regulators at the FCC or NTIA. To provide some balance, monitors should also include representatives of private carriers, equipment vendors, and large end users. Second, the

---

[10]Similarly, when the British started to deregulate their telecommunications market some years ago, they often looked to former employees of the old telecommunications monopoly to staff Oftel, the organization established to oversee the market's development. Anyone who knew enough about telecommunications to be valuable to Oftel almost had to have been an employee of the national monopoly at one time or another.

new monitors should be housed in a single agency rather than in the overlapping agencies that now deal with telecommunications matters. Other government interests in telecommunications markets should be brought within a streamlined FCC.

The most important way to ensure that we do not end up with more regulation in the name of free markets is to give the interim monitoring agency a definite, limited life span of two to three years' duration. The charter of the monitoring organization should include a provision making it difficult to extend the agency's authority beyond that period. Delaying the agency's sunset might require a two-thirds majority of both the House and Senate, for example.

During the transition, a phased approach to deregulation might be appropriate. Specific sunset dates could be established for particular laws and regulations, allowing the government's role and the FCC to shrink in anticipated steps, until finally the agency is closed. This planned approach, preferably written into law, would put everyone in the telecommunications markets on notice about where deregulation was headed and how it would get there. A similar approach was used in the case of airline deregulation with some success.

That leaves open the question of what the streamlined FCC would be doing in the first place. The quick answer is: as little as possible beyond the paperwork necessary to repeal telecommunications rules, regulations, and laws. I envision the new FCC as a small agency with a few hundred employees with only those powers necessary to respond to short-term problems.

The transitional FCC might be in the position to identify markets where temporary subsidies would be in order, for example. If prices for basic telephone service rise in some markets so that large numbers of the elderly and infirm are forced to disconnect their telephones over a short period of time, the FCC could provide temporary subsidies while the situation was studied.[11] Existing policies have led the sick and elderly to believe that the government will guarantee them communications services at very low prices, no matter what the real cost of the service is. Many persons have made important decisions based on that implicit promise. Although

---

[11]For those receiving subsidies, the inability to pay is critical. For some reason, it is often assumed that minimal services should be provided to the disabled and the elderly even if they are wealthy.

adjustments would need to be made in the long run, people cannot be let down overnight. The important point, however, is that subsidies would be provided for charitable reasons, not for redistributive ones.

The new agency would have no powers to address so-called unfair competition, nor would it be able to take steps to ensure that the poor had access to the same communications services as the rich. The streamlined FCC might, however, provide technical assistance in establishing markets for spectrum rights and other new property rights that would emerge as the result of market reform.

As the transition to a free market proceeds, disputes would no doubt arise within local communities and in the telecommunications industry. In such cases, the FCC might serve as an adviser or arbitrator, helping to resolve disputes. The technical talent, even in a streamlined FCC, would put it in an excellent position to fulfill that role on a formal or an informal basis. Disputes could also be settled in the courts, of course, but that would obviously require much more time. Arbitration by a technically competent panel formed as part of the transitional FCC would significantly reduce costs, in terms of both time and other resources. As with all its functions, however, arbitration by the FCC would be on an entirely voluntary basis—the agency staff would speak only when spoken to.

An Ongoing Role for the Government?

Of course, resolving disputes and the need for technical advice would not disappear with open markets in the telecommunications industry. Once the markets have had a chance to develop, however, those services could be provided by the private sector—by professional arbitrators, engineers, and consultants. The only reason for employing a government agency in the first place is that most of the necessary resources are currently found within the government, and operating with a stripped-down agency may be more efficient in the short run.

Even in a laissez-faire world, the government would have a role to play in keeping the telecommunications industry on track. But that role would have more to do with the traditional functions of government and far less to do with the special role that government has taken on with regard to the telecommunications industry. In the end, the only legitimate role for government is enforcing property rights and facilitating the definition of those rights where necessary. That is mostly a job for the courts, although the legislative and executive branches also have a small role to play.

Replacing the current morass of conflicting laws, rules, and regulations with a rigorous system of property rights would allow the communications infrastructure to flourish. Consumers and businesses would receive the services they need and want rather than the services the government thinks they ought to have. And with a property-rights approach we would have far less to worry about in terms of our First Amendment rights, as the new technologies break through the bounds of the old regulatory categories.

Index

About the Author

Lawrence Gasman is president of Communications Industry Researchers Inc., a management consulting firm specializing in technology and market forecasting for the telecommunications industry. He is the editor and publisher of *Broadband Networks and Applications Newsletter* and *Multimedia Networking Newsletter*, a columnist, and lectures widely on communications technology. He holds advanced degrees from the London School of Economics and the London Business School.

Cato Institute

Founded in 1977, the Cato Institute is a public policy research foundation dedicated to broadening the parameters of policy debate to allow consideration of more options that are consistent with the traditional American principles of limited government, individual liberty, and peace. To that end, the Institute strives to achieve greater involvement of the intelligent, concerned lay public in questions of policy and the proper role of government.

The Institute is named for *Cato's Letters*, libertarian pamphlets that were widely read in the American Colonies in the early 18th century and played a major role in laying the philosophical foundation for the American Revolution.

Despite the achievement of the nation's Founders, today virtually no aspect of life is free from government encroachment. A pervasive intolerance for individual rights is shown by government's arbitrary intrusions into private economic transactions and its disregard for civil liberties.

To counter that trend, the Cato Institute undertakes an extensive publications program that addresses the complete spectrum of policy issues. Books, monographs, and shorter studies are commissioned to examine the federal budget, Social Security, regulation, military spending, international trade, and myriad other issues. Major policy conferences are held throughout the year, from which papers are published thrice yearly in the *Cato Journal*. The Institute also publishes the quarterly magazine *Regulation*.

In order to maintain its independence, the Cato Institute accepts no government funding. Contributions are received from foundations, corporations, and individuals, and other revenue is generated from the sale of publications. The Institute is a nonprofit, tax-exempt, educational foundation under Section 501(c)3 of the Internal Revenue Code.

CATO INSTITUTE
1000 Massachusetts Ave., N.W.
Washington, D.C. 20001